WHITETAIL SECRETS
VOLUME FIVE

HUNTING THE CANADIAN GIANT

RUSSELL THORNBERRY

DERRYDALE PRESS

Lyon, Mississippi

WHITETAIL SECRETS

VOLUME FIVE, HUNTING THE CANADIAN GIANT

Published by the Derrydale Press, Inc. under the direction of:

Douglas C. Mauldin, President and Publisher

Craig Boddington, Series Editor

Sue Goss Griffin, Series Manager

Lynda Bell Taylor, Administrator

David Baer, Illustrator

Kirby J. Kiskadden, Designer

Cover: color photo by Ian McMurchy-World's Record Buck

Frontispiece: Russell Thornberry with a fine Saskatchewan Whitetail.

Frontispiece photo by Russell Thornberry

Inquiries should be addressed to the Derrydale Press, Inc., P.O. Box 411, Lyon, Mississippi 38645, Telephone 601-624-5514, Fax 601-627-3131

ISBN 1-56416-155-2

2 4 6 8 9 7 5 3 1

Printed in the United States of America on acid-free paper.

DEDICATION

To my wife Sharleen my Canadian treasure.

TABLE OF CONTENTS

EDITOR'S FOREWORD..1

CHAPTER 1
The Birth of an Industry 5

CHAPTER 2
Booking a Canadian Whitetail Hunt 19

CHAPTER 3
Travel Tips for Canada-Bound Hunters..........................29

CHAPTER 4
British Columbia 35

CHAPTER 5
Alberta...51

CHAPTER 6
Saskatchewan 71

CHAPTER 7
Manitoba 89

CHAPTER 8
The Cold Hard Facts About
Canadian Whitetail Hunting...107

CHAPTER 9
Subtle Secrets for Moving Deer 139

CHAPTER 10
Antler Rattling Tips for Canada....................................165

CHAPTER 11
Canadian Whitetail Rifles:
Mastering the Long Shots 181

CHAPTER 12
Canadian Whitetail Rifles:
Thicket Rifles...197

ACKNOWLEDGEMENTS

A very special thanks to Gary Tipper for his contribution to the chapter on British Columbia; to Rob Manley for his contribution to the Saskatchewan chapter; and to Rod Lehmann for his contribution to the Manitoba chapter.

Russell Thornberry

EDITOR'S FOREWORD

In our hunting world of the latter 20th Century Russell Thornberry accomplished something that seems almost impossible. Almost single-handedly he founded the Canadian whitetail hunting industry as we know it today—and he discovered the market to support it. No, Russ Thornberry did not "discover" Canada's big whitetails. Through the '50's and '60's Saskatchewan was the place to go for big bucks, pure and simple. But then American hunters were banned from Saskatchewan's southern zones, and her great deer were literally forgotten. As southern deer herds exploded, Texas emerged as the key trophy state, and it spawned America's first generation of whitetail fanatics.

Russ Thornberry was one of those fanatics, and he found himself in the right place at the right time. He was among the first outsiders to take notice of Alberta's big deer but, more important, he understood what they were and what to do with them. Starting in the early '70's, he guided and outfitted for Alberta whitetails—and did a fine job of publicizing them as well.

Russell Thornberry had the good sense, good fortune, and plain blind luck to know what a good whitetail looked like—and then to pitch up in Alberta before anybody else really figured out what a fabulous resource they had in those big northern bucks. It was partly accidental. After receiving an honorable discharge from the U.S. Army in 1965, Thornberry started what might have been a very successful singing career. In 1968 he lost his voice while doing a USO tour, and back in Los Angeles a doctor suggested he needed to get out of the smog to clear his sinuses. He headed to Canada to visit the only Canadian he knew. While there he was offered a contract with MCA records, plus a television show and solo concert opportunities. Naturally he stayed—partly for the great hunting opportunities. In fact, he stayed until 1990!

It was in the '70's, when I was a fledgling editor and Russ a fledgling writer, that we first crossed paths. Even 20 years ago Russell Thornberry was one of America's most knowledgeable whitetail experts. Back then we hadn't seen nothin' yet!

Fortunately for all of us Russell Thornberry wasn't the kind of guy who wanted to keep either the market or his accumulated knowledge all to himself. He is the founder and a past president of the Alberta Whitetail Outfitters Association, and as a writer has contributed to virtually every sporting publication in North America. He is perhaps best known as one of our most accomplished antler rattling experts, often the subject of his excellent whitetail seminars and the thrust of his book *The Art and Science of Rattling Whitetail Deer.* His other books include two volumes of humor: *Bucks, Bulls and Belly Laughs,* and *Dances With Turtles.*

These days he serves as Executive Editor of *Buckmasters' Whitetail Magazine,* and manages to find time to do a bit of hunting as well. Although whitetails remain his passion, he has hunted most North American big game and has travelled as far afield as Mongolia. With 35 years of whitetail hunting behind him and more than 25 years in pursuit of Canada's big bucks, Thornberry is truly a legend among modern whitetail hunters and clearly the only choice to write this volume about Canada's Giants.

But I'll tell you something most of you probably don't know about Russell Thornberry. Truth is he missed his calling. As a youngster his dream was to become a country western singer. I've heard him sing, and he could have done it. He's just as good at that as he is at everything else he attempts. But whitetails got in his way and in his blood, and as hunters we're all the more rich for it. So let's go hunting Canadian Giants with Russell Thornberry, a giant of a whitetail hunter and a great guy besides.

Craig Boddington

A scene like this would lead one to believe whitetails are plentiful in Canada. They are not. They congregate around available food, but in actuality deer densities in Canada are much lower than in most U.S. whitetail range. (Photo by Randy Bean)

a smaller deer at lesser range. I grew up believing everything was big in Texas, but in Canada the hunter really must think *big*!

During the early '70's, while I was pioneering a virtually unknown industry in nonresident whitetail hunting, I was also pioneering a career in outdoor writing. So, much of what I experienced as an Alberta whitetail outfitter found its way into print in a variety of North American hunting magazines. This Alberta exposure kindled the interest of American trophy whitetail *aficianados* and undoubtedly hastened the growth of the fledgling whitetail hunting industry in Alberta—and, subsequently, throughout western Canada. Perhaps to a fault. In a matter of less than a decade it seemed every man who owned a pickup truck was suddenly a whitetail guide and/or outfitter. The nonresident interest in Alberta as a whitetail hotspot quickly caused this industry to outgrow itself.

In those days anyone could be a whitetail guide anywhere in the province of Alberta. The Alberta government didn't even know how many or who the outfitters were or where they were hunting. The fact was that there were many so-called outfitters who didn't know a good whitetail from a hole in the ground. They were simply band-wagoning onto a young and vulnerable industry at the expense of many American hunters who had stars in their eyes but little real knowledge about what to expect when they got to the promised land.

Eventually, because of the "boom town" nature of the whitetail industry, the government had to get involved. A few easily accessible hunting areas with a reputation for producing exceptional bucks were overcrowded with outfitters and American hunters, and that began to aggravate the resident hunters and landowners. It didn't do much to perpetuate good will between Albertans and Americans. Even though those Americans came to Alberta with the best of intentions, they were often under the direction of less-than-scrupulous guides and outfitters. In the end it was Americans who took the brunt of resident animosity.

In 1990 the Alberta government pulled the reins in on the entire outfitting industry and allocated a specific number of nonresident permits in each wildlife management unit. This forced nonresident whitetail hunting to spread out over the province instead of concentrating in a few congested areas. Now outfitters were identified and licensed, allocated permits for nonresident hunters, and told that if they didn't toe the line they stood to lose their outfitting opportunity. Outfitters had to be bonded and were required to carry liability insurance. In other words, the industry was forced to grow up.

Although there were many growing pains in the process, this government control saved the life of outfitting in Alberta. Outfitters were forced to explore new areas, which they might never have done otherwise. The result for the nonresident hunter couldn't be better. Now his outfitter/guide has something to lose if he doesn't take care of business in a professional manner. More new whitetail turf has been cultivated and as many high-quality, uncrowded whitetail hunting opportunities exist today as when I was the only whitetail outfitter in eastern Alberta. The storm has passed and professional hunting in Alberta has been restored to a high degree of integrity.

Alberta's neighboring provinces, Saskatchewan and British Columbia, watched the nonresident whitetail interest blossom and soon hung up their own shingles. Today top-quality prairie whitetail hunts are available in B.C., Alberta, Saskatchewan, and Manitoba. Never have there been more great trophies than there are in western Canada today. Farmland is continually eating its way into the northern boreal forests of western Canada, creating new habitat. And in these areas where new ground is being broken you will find the strongest genetics possible.

Western Canadian winters guarantee predictable winterkills about every 10 years. This constant paring factor keeps western Canadian deer herds from ever reaching the carrying capacity of their habitat base. It also keeps the gene pool from stagnating. The harsh reality of Canadian winters mean fewer "fish in the bowl," so to speak, but that also means great trophy deer.

It is a biological given that the best trophy-class bucks occur when the posture of the herd is on the incline, prior to reaching the carrying capacity of the habitat base. Because of new land being broken to the plow and predictable, regular winter-kill, the deer herd in western Canada stays in a perpetual posture of incline, or growth.

That is to say the deer herd is always moving upward and never levels off.

The key to the greatest whitetail hunting is to hunt where the maximum number of years have passed since the last severe winter-kill. When four or five years in a row pass without serious winter losses, the numbers of mature bucks increase dramatically. The incredible numbers of great bucks produced by Alberta, B.C., and Saskatchewan in recent years is because the deer herd has been building on six or seven mild winters in a row. The result is high numbers of deer in general, and higher numbers of mature bucks which will be great trophy animals. A hunter is wise to keep track of areas where winter-kills have recently occurred. It makes a dramatic difference in the prospects for a real wallhanger.

Although western Canada produces astounding numbers of Boone and Crockett whitetails (an average of about one in 600 bucks harvested in Alberta, British Columbia, and Saskatchewan) the greater attraction is the awesome numbers of bucks in the 160-class and over. These are great trophies even if they don't end up in the record book! Often Canadian bucks will gross-score more than the book minimum of 170 points, then "deduct out" because of odd points and lack of symmetry. But, as most of the hunters I know say, "That's Boone and Crockett's problem!" It's the high potential average that makes western Canada so appetizing to nonresident whitetail hunters. The prevailing nonresident's expectation is that he or she will probably bag the buck of a lifetime on a Canadian hunt. This is not unrealistic. More often than not, this expectation is fulfilled.

Some hard-core types who want a B&C buck or nothing come regularly to Canada, and some of them even realize

Darcy Stewart took this superb 214⅝ nontypical in Manitoba. Throughout Canada's big buck country monsters can turn up literally anywhere—and often do. (Photo by Randy Bean)

their dreams. But whether they bag a "book" buck or not, most sportsmen who hunt western Canada regularly know they are hunting the best B&C whitetail country in existence.

Today a whitetail hunt in any of the western Canadian provinces will average about $3000 for a week-long hunt, which should include transportation (in Canada, not airfare to get there), lodging, meals, guide service, caping of the trophy, etc. Some hunts cost more and others cost less, but you generally get what you pay for. Hunters should be cautious about bargain basement prices. Good outfitters are booked up at the going rate. Unusually low-cost hunts generally spell lack of experience.

Until now I have been silent on eastern Canadian whitetail hunting. It's not because of lesser potential quality of deer. Nova Scotia and New Brunswick have produced some incredible trophies. But as an industry the eastern provinces are not geared to, nor do they produce, the numbers of top-end trophies comparable to the western provinces. This is due, in part, to the incredibly thick forests which limit visual contact with the deer. A friend of mine in New Brunswick bagged a typical Boone and Crockett buck with his shotgun. He admitted to me that, when he fired at the fleeing animal, all he could see was a white tail waving goodbye. Only when he recovered the deer did he realize it was a buck—and a giant buck at that!

Deer are harder to pattern and harder to see, and that makes eastern Canada a harder prospect for wallhangers. However, there is a very lively nonresident whitetail-hunting industry there. Traditionally the outfitters have not catered to hard-core trophy hunters, but rather have catered to American hunters who wanted a less expensive hunting opportunity which would render some venison for

The truly striking thing about Canadian whitetails is antler mass. Spreads aren't always impressive, and there are often odd points—but a 300-pound deer can grow a lot of antler. (Photo by Judd Cooney)

their efforts. Today some ardent outfitters in the east are taking up the trophy challenge and are producing some fine bucks.

November is the key month for big whitetails all across Canada. That's when the whitetails rut, and rifle seasons generally correspond with the rut. The peak of the rut usually occurs during the third week in November. The most dependable weeks to catch the primary rut are the second and third weeks of November. The first week of November can be good, as the pre-rut is in progress then and bucks are travelling continually in search of the first breeding does. However, if the weather is warm during that first week, the deer go entirely underground. The last week of the month can also be feast or famine. Warm weather, though unlikely, is the kiss of death and turns the bucks off like a light switch. Typically the last of the rut is still in progress then, and it is not unusual for the biggest buck of the season to pop up then. But for the highest odds, I recommend the second and third weeks of November.

Bow seasons generally begin in early September and run through October. In September the bucks are generally still tied to regular feeding schedules in fields. However, in early October, as they shift gears into preparation for the rut, they often also shift locations. There is a two-week lull in mid-October when big whitetails seem to vanish. Then, toward the end of October, as the pre-rut gets stronger, they begin to appear again. Nonresident bowhunters need time more than anything. In my opinion, it is unrealistic to come to Canada expecting to bag a real trophy buck in a week of hunting. Two weeks is much more realistic. The exception would be Saskatchewan, which allows baiting and thereby makes locating good bucks more dependable.

There has never been a better time than today to hunt British Columbia and the western prairie provinces. The deer population is at an all-time high, trophies abound, and the outfitting industry is healthier than it has ever been. The critical ingredients of age, nutrition, and ample food combine to make Canadian whitetails the envy of the continent. Now, having said all that, hearken to the reality that big bucks are seldom a pushover. Before you head for Canada, do your homework—and when you go, take all your luck with you. It's still very challenging hunting!

CHAPTER TWO

BOOKING A CANADIAN WHITETAIL HUNT

Nothing is more devastating than seeing a dream hunt go down the drain, but it happens all too often. Hunters, always expecting the best, learn the hard way that there is more than meets the eye when it comes to booking the right hunt with the right outfitter. Here are some keys the prospective Canadian whitetail hunter can employ to shake down his dream hunt before it turns out to be a nightmare.

First of all, determine how long the outfitter has been in business. There are many Canadian outfitters who advertise big and talk a good hunt but, in reality, lack experience. Ask for references from the past two or three seasons. If the outfitter cannot supply at least two years of references, hunter beware!

Outfitters will likely offer successful hunter references. The successful hunter is obviously going to be more positive about his hunt than an unsuccessful hunter. The unsuccessful hunter will tell you his opinion of the outfitter and his services based upon performance and effort made on his behalf. I recommend that the prospective hunter talk to as many *unsuccessful* hunters as possible. Get both sides of the story. If an unsuccessful hunter can praise his outfitter and vouch for his guides and services, you know you have heard the truth. A lucky hunter may step out the

Different outfitters use different methods. This guide likes to set up a ground blind, often a sound tactic. If you have strong preferences in hunting techniques, be sure to find out how your outfitter hunts. (Photo by Craig Boddington)

front door and bag a trophy, but that doesn't mean he has been hunting. A man who has been dependent upon his outfitter for the entire hunt will know if his investment was sound or not.

Success rate is very important so that the hunter may have a realistic expectation. If an outfitter avoids answering this question, then avoid him!

It is also important to establish what size deer were killed in the success rate offered. If you are a trophy hunter, you want to know how many actual trophies were taken, not how many deer hit the ground. Some outfitters will slant the truth by quoting percentage of kill based on some deer that are far short of trophy status. Invest in some phone calls and talk to as many references as you can. You can't afford not to!

Determine the style and method of hunting the outfitter or guide service employs. This is a very important factor. Hunters tend to mentally project the style of hunting they use at home into the hunt they are buying. Then, when they arrive hundreds of miles from home, they find that everything is different. For example, a New Jersey hunter who particularly enjoys deer drives may expect that he will be hunting in that fashion on his whitetail hunt somewhere in the Northwest. When he arrives he finds that his outfitter will not employ deer drives. Perhaps the outfitter knows that the timber is too vast to successfully drive a big buck. He tells the hunter to take a stand in the river valley. The hunter doesn't like stands and the hunt goes sour.

When you plan to travel to Canada to hunt, talk to the outfitter about how you like to hunt and be sure that he is in agreement with your concepts before you arrive. If the method of hunting is as important as the quality of the deer you take, then knowing how you are going to hunt is of utmost importance.

It is wise for the travelling hunter to go with a flexible

These Alberta hunters scored three out of five (the sixth man is the outfitter). That's actually pretty good. When planning a Canadian hunt, you must understand that the buck of a lifetime might be yours—but success is not assured. (Photo by Craig Boddington)

and open mind because his personal preference of hunting technique may not make sense in another area. In any case, all this should be established in advance to avoid disappointment.

There are some Canadian outfitter/guides who really do not hunt in the true sense of the word. They simply ride around in trucks in hopes of seeing a buck. Naturally this

Winter is the limiting factor on Canadian whitetail, and a hard winter can knock the herd back for several years. When planning a hunt, find out how the winters have been in that exact area! (Photo by Judd Cooney)

is pure torture to a hunter who wants to see, feel, and smell every inch of the ground he hunts. Conversely, some hunters show up and demand a road hunt and the outfitter will not comply. Talk it out in advance and be sure you and your outfitter speak the same language.

Watch for hidden costs. Ask your outfitter what potential extras you might face. Some charge trophy fees on top of the hunt cost. In some cases provincial governments charge a trophy or export fee. Ask if the cost of the license is included or not. Inquire about the guide service, bedding, meals, transportation; and establish a specific time and place to rendezvous with your outfitter when you arrive in his area. Ask about exporting your cape, antlers, and meat if you so desire. Know exactly what services are provided and exactly how much it's going to cost. Some hunts appear to be a bargain until you look behind the scenes and suddenly find that every step you take adds on extra dollars.

This guide rattles from the ground while his bowhunter takes a stand. While two is often a crowd when hunting whitetails, this is a team effort that can pay off. (Photo by Charles Alsheimer)

Ask your outfitter to provide a comprehensive list of gear you will need for your hunt. A southern hunter planning a trip to Canada may find himself unable to obtain locally the proper clothing for a northern hunt. Time is needed to order equipment or clothing from a catalog house. What suits the occasion in south Texas will hardly suffice in the subzero temperatures of the northern Canadian whitetail range. Get that list and be sure you are prepared.

Ask the outfitter what factors rob his unsuccessful hunters of their success. If he is honest he will tell you what his unsuccessful hunters do, or don't do, that costs them their deer. Frozen firing pins are one example. By asking the right questions you might find it necessary to remove all the oil and grease from your rifle bolt before you go north to hunt. Knowing what to ask may keep you out of the ranks of the unsuccessful!

Ask the outfitter what rifle caliber he recommends. You may find that the light bullets you're using on 120-pound deer are not suitable for deer twice that size and more. Perhaps you hunt tight brush with a .30-30 at home. Now you're heading for Alberta where long shots are common. You might be better off with a 7mm magnum or a .270. A good outfitter will be able to recommend a sensible rifle for his area.

Beware of guaranteed hunts. No honest outfitter will guarantee your success on a trophy whitetail hunt. If he does, he is saying that he can speak for himself, the deer, *and* you! The only way to guarantee a hunt is to have the deer already hanging when the hunter arrives. No self-respecting hunter would be part of such a scheme.

Today, as never before, Canadian trophy whitetail hunting is in demand. There are those time-proven outfitters who are worth every penny they charge. But, unfortunately, for every reputable outfitter there is at least one who will let you down. Check to see if the outfitter you are con-

With deer densities fairly low, one of the most important things an outfitter can do for you is locate good sign where bucks are hanging out. (Photo by Craig Boddington)

sidering is in good standing with an outfitter organization in his province. Find out if he is personally going to be present when you are in his camp. Things tend to be more as advertised when the boss is around!

Don't let your own lack of attention to detail be the reason you are disappointed in your hunt of a lifetime. Whitetail deer hunting is a never-ending matter of details. It follows that booking a Canadian hunt for a trophy buck demands equal attention to the fine print. Every question you get answered before you leave home ups your odds of success.

CHAPTER THREE

TRAVEL TIPS FOR CANADA-BOUND HUNTERS

Canada is indeed our neighbor to the north, a primary trade partner, and historically one of the United States' closest allies and friends. Travel in Canada is every bit as simple as travel in the U.S.—sometimes more so. But it *is* a different country, and American hunters must keep this simple and often not-so-obvious fact in mind.

Clearing Canadian Customs

Every American hunter who is planning a hunting trip to Canada should be aware of how Canadian firearms and ammunition laws affect him or her. First and most important is the "NO HANDGUNS" law. A visiting hunter may not enter Canada with a handgun, nor is hunting with one permitted in Canada. This is a law that Canadian authorities take very seriously; those who are unaware of it or choose to ignore it inevitably have their handguns confiscated at the border—and that's the best result.

At present a hunter may enter Canada with one or more hunting rifles and/or shotguns as long as they are not fully automatic. The cartridge capacity of big game rifles may not exceed five rounds, including combined capacity of magazine and chamber. Shotguns are limited to a three-round capacity. A hunter may bring a total maximum of 200 rounds of ammunition when entering Canada.

Re-entering the U.S. from Canada

Upon exiting Canada American hunters must be certain they have the necessary Canadian provincial export document for the animals being exported to the U.S. This documentation must be presented to U.S. customs upon re-entering the United States. The customs officials will have you fill out a U.S. Fish and Wildlife declaration; it's a very simple process provided you have the proper Canadian hunting license and export documents. Your Canadian outfitter/guide should assist you fully in obtaining the required export documents.

It is far simpler to take your trophy (cape, antlers, and meat) with you when you travel rather than have it shipped at a later date—and far less costly. Properly packaged antlers and skins, and even meat, can easily be checked as baggage on airlines and will travel with you. However, should any parts of wildlife be shipped to you at a later date, they must also be cleared through customs and the U.S. Fish and Wildlife Service. You may use the U.S. Fish and Wildlife office nearest your home, but even under the best of circumstances this will mean more time in transit and more shipping expense.

I always roll up my whitetail capes and freeze them before travelling. I take along a spare duffel bag and put the cape and antlers in it, then pack my insulated hunting garments around them for protection. The baggage storage compartments of airplanes stay so cold I have never experienced any problem with thawing of meat or capes. Again, freezing is the best option. In warmer weather, or

A sturdy guncase that will protect your firearms on the journey to Canada is essential. Even then, you should absolutely insist on checking your zero on arrival—it's too late when a good buck appears. (Photo by Craig Boddington)

if you have a few days before departure, salting the cape is another option. Salt draws the moisture out of the skin, and eventually it will dry stiff and hard. The catch is that freshly salted capes should not be frozen. The salt lowers the freezing temperature. Salt and dry *completely,* a time consuming process; or freeze. *Do not* mix the two methods.

A word of caution is advisable for those of you who want to take home some venison for the table. Freeze the venison and pack it in a suitcase or duffel bag but don't label it as frozen meat. Sadly, many of today's airline baggage handlers make a habit of stealing containers identified as carrying meat or other kinds of food. This is not idle speculation on my part. I have observed this many times and have been advised of the seriousness of the problem by airline employees.

Meat that is well-frozen and then insulated in your baggage should make the trip with no problem. Avoid dry ice if you're travelling by commercial aircraft—they will usually not carry it, and if you're using it you are obligated to tell them.

Speaking of obligations, you are legally required to declare that you have firearms. Don't travel with undeclared firearms—the penalties are severe these days. Your firearms and ammunition must be packed separately. Just put the ammunition in original factory containers, no more than five kilograms (about 11 pounds), in your duffel bag or suitcase. You should have no problems.

Firearms Proof of Origin

When returning to the U.S. from Canada it is not uncommon for U.S. Customs officials to ask the hunter to prove the origin of his firearm. If the hunter cannot prove the firearm was purchased in the U.S. the agent may confiscate the firearm in question. The solution is simple: Before leaving the United States visit the Customs office nearest your home—with your firearm, discretely cased—and fill out a Customs Form 4457, which will identify your firearm by serial number.

This is the same form used for any valuables to be taken abroad—cameras, watches, jewelry, etc. It takes just a few moments to fill out the form and have it stamped. It is not registration of the firearm; there is no duplicate of the form, and the original stays with you and is good forever.

If you cannot find time to obtain the form, a bill of sale is generally acceptable. Obviously you can expect fewer questions with American-made firearms, but if your rifle was made elsewhere far and away the safest and most hassle-free course is to obtain the Form 4457.

CHAPTER FOUR

BRITISH COLUMBIA

British Columbia is a rugged province, and can be realistically considered a trifle inhospitable for some species of wildlife and humans alike. Of course, from a human perspective, there are sought-after regions such as the sunny Okanagan, the lower mainland with the metropolis of Vancouver, and the retirement haven of southern Vancouver Island. These areas represent the heartbeat of the province, and by far support the bulk of human population and activity. Generally, the remainder of the population is concentrated in valleys, of which there are few relative to the surrounding mountains. Exceptions occur in the central plateau and the Rocky Mountain foothills of the northeast.

What bearing does a discussion of geography and demographics have on a chapter about whitetail deer? It provides a backdrop for an understanding of the range of the whitetail in B.C., as well as an understanding of the intense competition for the limited valley bottom land, critical as wildlife habitat, developed for human habitation, utilized for transportation and utility corridors, tilled for agriculture, and flooded for hydroelectric power generation. The latter use pre-empts all others, and is responsible for the greatest negative impact on whitetail deer in the province.

The estimated 40,000 to 50,000 whitetail deer in British Columbia, with a fawn-to-adult ratio of 50:100, occur in two distinct areas. Both are extensions of populations from

Russell Thornberry displays the mounted head of British Columbia's top-scoring nontypical, a wonderful buck scoring 245⅞. Although whitetails are considered relative newcomers to B.C., James Brewster shot this buck on the Elk River in 1905!

other jurisdictions. The largest numbers occur in the Okanagan and Kootenay Regions, and are contiguous with the vast pool of whitetail deer in the United States.

The climate of southern B.C. is comparatively moderate. In conjunction with relatively large north-south valleys; mixed coniferous forest interspersed with openings; and small, rich, riparian areas (areas of vegetation influenced by water) provide the requirement of whitetail deer in the form of food, water, and shelter. Native forage species are

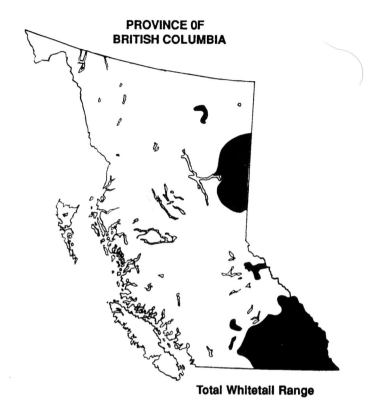

**PROVINCE OF
BRITISH COLUMBIA**

Total Whitetail Range

primarily shrubs like red- and yellow-stem ceanothus, saskatoon, red osier dogwood, maple, willow, Oregon grape, and kinnikinnik. Douglas fir needles form up to one-third of the whitetails' winter diet, and the fresh, green shoots of grasses and forbs are critical in the spring and early summer. Alfalfa and other forage crops augment native forage supply. Conflicts occur in some areas where deer browse on fruit-bearing trees and shrubs in orchards or when heavy concentrations of deer graze alfalfa fields.

Winter is the major factor limiting whitetail populations. Low elevation winter range, in short supply due to topog-

PROVINCE OF BRITISH COLUMBIA

**Greatest Whitetail
Population Density**

raphy and the myriad conflicts alluded to earlier, is critical
to survival. Mature Douglas fir forests provide a canopy,
which intercepts snow, allowing deer to move and forage
freely. South and west-facing slopes, where forage-rich
openings often occur, are similarly accessible due to the effect of the low winter sun. Long, cold winters with deep
snows such as occurred in 1968, 1972, and 1977 drive
numbers down—and emphasize importance of winter
ranges in good condition. Additionally, predation dampens
populations in localized areas. Coyotes, cougars, black

**PROVINCE OF
BRITISH COLUMBIA**

**Best Whitetail
Trophy Area**

bear, lynx, and bobcats are present in viable numbers and
reduce the recruitment of fawns to adults.

The other major concentration of whitetail deer occur in
the Peace River area of northeastern B.C. This is an intrusion of prairie and foothill terrain—and whitetail deer—
into B.C. from Alberta. The snow depths of this area are
moderated by the rain shadow effect of the northern Rocky
Mountains, as well as by warm weather which periodically
pushes up from the south, creating a warming trend long
referred to as a chinook.

Kevin Woods of Michigan bagged this mountain whitetail while hunting with outfitter Carmen Dempsey out of Golden, B.C. Dempsey finds his whitetails along the Columbia and Kootenay Rivers in southeastern B.C. (Photo by Carmen Dempsey)

Native forage species are less diverse here, but due to the area's productivity are very abundant. Saskatoon, red osier dogwood, and willow are the staples, with grasses and forbs again being critical in the spring. Agricultural crops such as hay and cereal grains are available and provide additional forage. Mild winters have allowed the whitetail populations to expand their numbers in what is essentially the northern limit of their distribution.

On the plains, where topographic variation is minimal, whitetail deer distribution is influenced by the vegetative mosaic created by cereal crop agriculture. Mixed conifer-aspen forests provide the required visual relief, snow relief, and thermal cover. In the foothills, steep south-facing slopes are critical as winter range, since the solar radiation reduces snow depths to allow easier movement and access to forage. Predators include wolves, coyotes, and black bear, with coy-

Signs like this huge rub leave little doubt that a buck worth pursuing is in the area. This was but one of dozens of rubs the author found while hunting in the Fort St. John region.

otes as the most abundant. Wolf numbers are limited by predator control because of conflict with livestock.

The reader should note that the following statistical information concerning whitetail deer in B.C. is heavily biased to the Kootenay Region, which supports 62 percent of the province's total of that species. In 1987 it was estimated that 4242 bucks were harvested, along with 658 does and 99 fawns, for a provincial total of 4999 whitetail deer harvested. The success rate was 22 percent, or 30.61 days/kill for resident hunters. It is not broken down by type of arm. A total of 23,001 resident licenses were sold, and the additional number of nonresident licenses is not available. Prior to 1988, although regulations were set separately, it was only necessary to purchase a "deer" license, which covered blacktail, mule, and whitetail deer.

In relative terms, hunting regulations have become more complex and more restrictive over time. This has occurred because of greater hunting pressure, and the impact of other factors such as habitat loss, on whitetail deer populations. The complex seasons and the Limited Entry Hunt, a hunt which only B.C. residents can apply for and participate in, are designed to distribute hunter effort and harvest geographically as well as across the sexes of the deer population. In heavily-hunted areas such as the East Kootenay, the season has been shortened to end on November 15 in order to reduce the harvest of bucks made vulnerable by the rut and the onset of winter snows.

British Columbia is divided into five administrative regions for the purpose of managing and regulating the harvest of fish and wildlife. Regions may be composed of two or three sub-regions, which are, in turn, broken down into management units—which is the level at which whitetail deer regulations are currently set. In order to ensure a trouble-free hunt, the British Columbia Hunting Regulations Synopsis, printed annually and widely available throughout the province, should be consulted.

Nonresidents of B.C. hunting big game must be accompanied by a licensed B.C. guide, or by someone who qualifies under one of the required relationship categories. A nonresident of B.C. who is a resident of Canada may be accompanied by a B.C. resident, provided that the resident is a Canadian citizen and has obtained the required permit from the Ministry of Environment Regional Office in the Region the hunt will take place.

British Columbia has an active guide-outfitting industry, due both to the guide requirement mentioned above plus the demand for the wildlife species and wilderness experience available in this province. Few outfitters specialize in whitetail deer hunts, but most of them whose territories have an open season for whitetail provide their services for this purpose. The demand by nonresidents appears to be rising, so an increased number of guided whitetail deer hunts is anticipated. In time, certain outfitters may begin to focus more on whitetails and advertise that particular specialty.

With the opportunity for larger, heavier wildlife species which require both energy and penetration to ensure clean, and in some cases safe, kills, it is not altogether unusual for the one-rifle hunter to be somewhat overgunned when hunting whitetails with his .300 or .338 magnum—which are quite appropriate for elk, moose, or bear. Magnum rifle users also assert that the greater retained energy and less bullet drop at long ranges provides them with a better chance to score a vital hit. This could prove important in some of the more open whitetail deer habitats found in parts of the East Kootenay, Okanagan, and Peace sub-regions.

British Columbia ranks fourth in Canada for the number of typical whitetail bucks in the records, following Manitoba, Alberta, and Saskatchewan. The latter province holds by far the most records. It now appears as though the Kootenay Region may be releasing its traditional hold on records from B.C., with the Okanagan sub-region and the Peace sub-region producing some impressive trophies in recent years.

The hunter has a number of decisions to make in choosing his trophy area. Some of these are: The availability of a guide-outfitter for nonresidents; the location of a relative

Bob Kress of Fort St. John displays three of his excellent B.C. whitetail trophies. The deer aren't numerous up there—but they're expanding their range rapidly, and an expanding herd offers among the best trophy potential. (Photo by Bob Kress)

or friend for a nonresident Canadian; the type of terrain and vegetation he/she prefers hunting in; whether other species may be hunted on the same trip; and distance to travel. The latter may be a point weighing against the Peace River country, where a great potential to produce trophy bucks is just now being recognized. It's a long ways north, but a serious trophy hunter would be well-advised to bite the bullet and go the extra distance. My hunting experience in the Fort St. John region, along the Peace River drainage, convinced me that though the whitetail population is low (estimated 10,000) the trophy potential is as good as any I've seen anywhere in western Canada.

During the fall of 1993 I hunted the Peace River drainage with my longtime friend Ray Jackson, of Horseshoe Creek Outfitters in Charlie Lake, B.C. Jackson (a Mississippi boy originally) settled in the area primarily because of the trophy deer he found there.

My decision to pursue trophy whitetails in the area was prompted by a visit I made to Fort St. John several years ago when I was invited by the North Peace Rod and Gun Club to come and present a whitetail hunting seminar to their membership.

The bucks they had hanging on the walls at that meeting looked like the whitetail hall of fame! It was apparent when talking to the hunters that the whitetail was the new kid on the block. This area was, and still is to a great extent, the domain of mule deer. It's true that the whitetail is a newcomer to the region, but there are some distinct advantages to that. Biologists agree that the greatest trophy potential among whitetail bucks occurs when the animals move into a new range. The reason is that the gene pool is at its strongest when this occurs. So, while numbers are not high, quality is! The breaking of land for farming and ranching along the Peace River has lured the herd west from Alberta.

If there is a down side to trophy hunting in B.C., it's that they close the season in the middle of November, just before the rut breaks loose. It's heartbreaking to have to abandon the hunt just before it really peaks, but the long-term plan makes sense. For now, Canada's western-most province is trying to build the herd, so some regulated protection is definitely necessary to accomplish this goal.

Most whitetails are shot in two distinct time periods. The first major harvest occurs during the week the season opens. Yearlings on their own for the first time are vulnerable, as are some of the older animals lulled into complacency by nine months of no hunting. The second major kill occurs as the arrival of winter triggers migration from summer range to winter range. Since the latter is relatively scarce, the animals are much more highly concentrated and therefore more frequently encountered by hunters than on summer range. Snow also makes them more visible. Additionally, the rut, which begins around the end of October and runs through November, causes substantial behavioral changes in whitetail bucks which make them more vulnerable.

Popular hunting methods are, for the most part, quite traditional. Still hunting predominates, since most hunters prefer moving, albeit extremely slowly, to sitting in a stand for long periods of time. Sitting requires a great deal of patience, particularly in cold or wet weather. Although still hunting is a relatively productive method of hunting most forest-dwelling big game species, stand hunting is probably more successful. The stand may be nothing more exotic than a tree, log, or stump—or may be as complex as a ground blind or treestand. Certain combinations of terrain and vegetation lend themselves to drives, with as few as two people participating. One acts as the "dog" and one as the shooter. Rattling is a hunting method which can, of course, only be practiced successfully during the rut and then best from a stand.

Most hunting of whitetails on native range occurs on Crown land (the Canadian equivalent of U.S. National Forests) in British Columbia, where over 90 percent of the land is under the control of the provincial government. Hunting from a stand with a good view of agricultural crop lands is the most common type of hunting which occurs on private land. Many landowners are receptive to this form of hunting upon obtaining permission, and may encourage it in some areas where damage to crops, particularly in orchards, is a problem.

British Columbians have long been exposed to nonresident hunters and the guiding industry. The relationship between resident and nonresident hunters is generally one of coexistence, which can become a bit thorny when one

While most of the thunder goes to provinces farther east, British Columbia actually offers equal trophy potential—but concentrated into smaller pockets because of its mountainous terrain.

encounters another in a favorite deer patch. However, animosity, if displayed at all, is usually reserved for a few mutterings about the guide's ancestry—or vice versa. The guiding industry in B.C. is respectable—and well-recognized by other businessmen as a healthy source of income. Additionally, tourism is a major industry. Service people as well as merchants endeavor to buttress the province's reputation as a scenic and friendly destination. The positive marketing attitude is evident all the way to the legislature in Victoria.

The future for whitetail deer in British Columbia is optimistic. Attention to the species is increasing, which cannot but help to increase success in habitat protection, habitat enhancement, and population management. The land use conflicts will continue, but hopefully the major impacts have already occurred: the dams have been built and the development boom of the 1970's is over. Political and land-use philosophies in the late 1980's became more tempered with a respect for wildlife and its rights as a user of the land. The whitetail deer is an adaptable creature which may, if worse comes to worst, survive in spite of us. In the meantime, it will continue to provide countless hours of enjoyment for both hunters and non-hunters alike.

- Resident whitetail hunter success rate: 1 out of 3 hunters with an average of 25 hunter-days per deer harvested.
- Total whitetail harvest in 1993: 8900
- Total whitetail hunters in 1993: 28,000
- Buck harvest, 1993: 6665
- Doe harvest, 1993: 2591
- Top 4 whitetail-producing areas:
  1. East Kootenay Region
  2. Okanagan Region
  3. West Kootenay Region
  4. Peace River Region
- 1994 Archery Season: 7 to 9-day season (depending upon area), early September.
- Rifle Season: September 10 to mid-November.
- Cost of 1994 nonresident license: $145 Canadian funds.
- Cost of 1994 nonresident whitetail tag: $75 each Canadian funds.
- Nonresident bag limits: 1 to 3 deer, depending on region.

FOR INFORMATION:

For hunting information or listings of guides and outfitters, contact:

British Columbia Ministry of Environment
Wildlife Branch
780 Blanchard Street
Victoria, British Columbia
Canada V8V 1X4

CHAPTER FIVE

ALBERTA

Alberta undoubtedly offers one of the greatest opportunities available today for a true record-class, monster whitetail. It might also be described as one of the best bets on the continent for getting skunked. Actually, both statements describe hunting for real trophy whitetails in this western Canadian province.

Of approximately 20,000 whitetail bucks harvested annually, from 12 to 20 or more will score high enough for inclusion into the coveted annals of the Boone and Crockett records. I am aware of at least 150 B&C-quality heads taken in Alberta, the majority of which have never been officially scored. I would not doubt there are many more than that.

The spotlight has been focussed on Alberta over the last 15 years because of the large animals being taken there, but when whitetail mania hits a fever pitch the facts are sometimes distorted. Some hunters come to Alberta expecting to find a monster buck behind every tree. That's not the case. Excellent trophies are present in unusually good numbers—but they are still a challenge to even the best deer hunter. I will attempt to shed some light on trophy whitetail hunting in Alberta for those who might be considering a trip to the promised land.

Selecting the right area in which to hunt big whitetails in Alberta is more a matter of where the deer are huntable

Don McGarvey's 1991 Alberta buck, the new Pope & Young number two typical. (Photo by Dan Wiles)

than where the big deer exist. Trophy class bucks are found in every part of the province, but they are more huntable in a few main areas. By "huntable" I mean where the hunter's odds of seeing such a deer are practical and realistic based on visibility and geography.

I have often said in jest that if whitetails occupied the lofty domain of the bighorn sheep they would be invinci-

ALBERTA

Total Whitetail Range

ble. Back in the fall of '81 I knew of at least five whitetail bucks which were spotted in the Alberta Rockies at elevations of 6000 feet. In one case a whitetail buck was spotted above timberline amidst a group of bighorn ewes. The buck was reported to have been kicking and hooking at the ewes with his antlers and appeared to be generally harassing them.

The whitetails have moved into the mountains in Alberta and are doing well there. There are some tremendous bucks in the high country now—but that does not mean they are easily available to hunters. This is the point I am trying to make about being available. Whitetails also live in the bald prairies of southeastern Alberta, where the antelope now

ALBERTA

**Greatest Whitetail
Population Density
Most Trophies Taken
(to 1994)**

share their habitat, and where the prairie bison once roamed. I would not choose to hunt seriously for a monster-class whitetail in the prairie any more than I would in the Rockies. They are all but unapproachable there.

Most hunters will agree that the eastern corridor of the province from the Cold Lake region south to the Neutral Hills is the best opportunity for hunting trophy whitetails. To define the most huntable whitetail area of Alberta, one could trace a block on an Alberta map using the Saskatchewan border as the eastern boundary. The northern boundary would run east from Cold Lake to Whitecourt.

ALBERTA

Prime Whitetail
Forest Fringe Area

The western boundary would run south from Whitecourt to Cochrane, west of Calgary. And, finally, the southern boundary would be marked by a line from Cochrane east to Oyen, back on the Saskatchewan border. Again I stress this block of territory does not define all of Alberta's great trophy potential, but rather the area where they can be hunted systematically. Within this large block of roughly 45,000 to 50,000 square miles a book whitetail is possible anywhere.

In Alberta a trophy does not necessarily mean a B&C animal. Some of the tangle-horned bucks of this area will not score well but will be more impressive by far than a great

Ed Koberstein's 1991 buck was originally believed to be a new world record, but its score was disqualified and the final score is yet unknown. Whatever it is, it's a great buck.

Neil Morin capped off 1991 with this province record scoring 278⅞, the fifth largest nontypical on record. This buck was taken far north of the typical trophy areas.

number of deer which qualify for B&C. Irregular antlers are common in this area.

The terrain in this vast area is a mixture of farm and ranch land. Some is privately owned land and some is government land, called Crown Land, similar to National Forests in the

Doug Klinger's 277⅝ buck was taken along the Battle River near Hardisty, Alberta, in 1976.

This Alberta monster was taken by Jerry Froma in 1984, near Barrhead. It's the current number 11 in B&C.

U.S. Sprawling stands of aspen and cottonwood, mixed with pine and spruce, border wheat, barley, oat, and alfalfa fields. These hay and grain crops bordering large tracts of timber are magnetic to whitetails. As long as the grain or stubble remains, whitetails will frequent the fields.

Some credit the large body size of Alberta whitetails to the availability of grain crops, but it is interesting to note that they get just as big where they have absolutely no access to any crops at all. In the sand hills of central eastern Alberta, where gnarled aspens cover the landscape and the silver willow and snowberry bushes constitute the mainstay of the whitetail's diet, huge bucks are taken each season.

This mixture of grain farming and rolling hills of stunted aspen trees is perhaps the prime huntable whitetail habitat of Alberta. Four major river valleys carve their way through this region. The North Saskatchewan, Battle, Red Deer, and South Saskatchewan Rivers comprise the finest whitetail habitat Alberta has to offer. The Battle and North Saskatchewan Rivers are both excellent potential trophy areas and the thick combination of willow, dogwood, and alders creates an impenetrable refuge for the deer. Likewise, the Red Deer and South Saskatchewan produce excellent habitat. These two rivers flow through open prairie and offer the mainstay of whitetail habitat in the far southeastern corner of the province. All four of these river channels are dotted with islands which also furnish excellent habitat for the whitetails.

While the prime whitetail hunting area of Alberta offers unsurpassed habitat and deer, much of the land is criss-crossed with road allowances which form a huge grid system. The roadways occur at one-mile and two-mile intervals running north, south, east, and west. The unfortunate part is that there are very few tracts of land owned by one owner. The buck you may be hunting may travel through several different pieces of property owned by several landowners. There is little control of the deer where the land is divided into such small individual parcels. To complicate matters even more, the landowners may own several quarter-sections (160 acres), none of which adjoin each other. Trespass laws in Alberta have traditionally been taken lightly; if the land is unoccupied someone will likely hunt there regardless of what signs may say. This random and relatively uncontrolled hunting makes it hard to hunt a specific deer with confidence unless you manage to find a key area which has some geographical boundaries which stop vehicles. Some of the river valleys mentioned here do

Dan Dwernychuk's 241⅛ nontypical, taken in 1984, is the largest Canadian buck taken by a bowhunter to date.

Stephen Jansen's 204⅔ typical, taken in 1967, is Alberta's highest-scoring typical, at the time coming very close to the world record.

create places where the traffic cannot drive and these are areas where hunting can still be controlled.

Now that the restructuring of the whitetail outfitting industry has pushed outfitters into more remote parts of the province, it is possible to hunt lightly pressured areas with little competition. But such areas will usually be along the northern or western boundary of the huge block previously described.

At the present time it is against the law to buy or sell the right of access for the purpose of hunting on private land in Alberta. There is reason to believe that the pressure on private lands for the purpose of hunting will bring about a change in that law. The future of the habitat for the white-tail deer in this area will ultimately depend on the realizing a specific dollar value for deer and deer hunting.

Hunting methods for Alberta whitetails depend on several factors. In the past, most hunting for deer in Alberta was done from vehicles. Even today, hunters who wish to still-hunt or hunt from a blind must find an area with some geographical barriers to block roaming vehicles. Once such a place is located, still-hunting, blinds, or treestand hunting can be excellent. Still-hunting is an uphill business for big bucks in Alberta, as it is everyplace else, but hunting from a ground blind or treestand can pay off. Outfitters who do their homework and place stands and blinds in strategic areas have excellent hunter success rates on true trophies.

Rattling antlers can be productive in Alberta, but this method is also dependent on locating an area where hunter traffic is quiet. There is also a very real hazard to rattling antlers in any area where hunting is not completely controlled. In such areas there is the possibility of rattling up an unexpected deer hunter instead of a deer. At best, rattling antlers in Alberta cannot compare with places such as Texas because the population of deer is so much lower and so much less dense that the sound simply does not reach as many ears per rattling attempt. My best success was four bucks in 12 attempts during the course of the seasons.

The rut occurs in mid to late November in Alberta. According to fetus studies, it peaks about the 26th of that month. Hunting at this time, like hunting the rut anywhere, raises the odds for success on big bucks. In my many years of hunting whitetails in Alberta I have seldom seen a real monster a second time, although I have seen many huge bucks. The hunter who wants a great buck

Alberta guides Shane Hansen and Cliff Hanna found these two huge bucks locked together. The larger scored over 210 points; the smaller, a nine-pointer, would have made B&C as a typical if he'd had a matching point.

must be prepared to shoot him where he sees him. There are very few second chances and *no* next times.

In some areas shots may be long, so hunters are advised to use rifles and calibers they can shoot with confidence out to 400 yards. I would not recommend a caliber less than .25 for Alberta whitetails. It has been my experience that more big bucks are seen at ranges in excess of 250 yards than at less. Magnum firepower is worthwhile for the sake of bullet performance at long range, but I suggest that good, expanding 180-grain bullets are as heavy as needed.

In Alberta, as in all the Canadian prairie provinces, November temperatures may range from +60 degrees F. to –30 degrees F. The colder weather is more desirable because it puts the deer on the move and snow makes deer much easier to see. The hunter should bring enough clothing to accommodate all the possibilities—for they may all occur in the same week. As is typical of whitetail hunting, a cold snap during the rut is like magic and the hunter will see deer everywhere. On the other hand, a warm November can test one's imagination and good humor!

Only in the last 15 years has the whitetail been recognized by resident Albertans as a world-class trophy. Most resident hunters were more interested in meat for the freezer than they were in turning down small bucks and waiting for a chance at the big fellow. This trend has changed as the popularity of the whitetail has increased and as more nonresident hunters come to Alberta to hunt them.

The future of whitetail hunting in Alberta has never been brighter for the nonresident hunter. Thanks to the somewhat painful restructuring of the entire guiding industry in recent years, hunting pressure is no longer confined to a few congested areas. Fly-by-night outfitters have been forced out of business, and the ones remaining are much more likely to serve the visiting hunter well. The trophy harvests of recent years prove the good ol' days of deer hunting in Alberta are still happening.

At present the bag limit for nonresident whitetail hunters is one animal of either sex in most wildlife management units. This animal may be taken during the bow or rifle seasons. Firearms are forbidden during the archery season, but bows may be used during the firearms season.

Ken Harris of Alabama bagged this dream buck while hunting Alberta's forest fringe with outfitter Neal Courtice. This is a great buck anyway—but look at the drop tine!

In either case the bowhunter requires a special archery stamp on his license.

Alberta's Best Whitetails

In the fall of 1991 Don McGarvey of Edmonton, Alberta arrowed the new Number Two typical Pope and Young record, scoring 199⅝. That same fall Ed Koberstein took an Alberta monster which was initially scored at 207 ²⁄₈, challenging the long-standing Boone and Crockett world record. Later the B&C officials disqualified the score, and as yet it has not been remeasured.

During that same incredible 1991 season yet another staggering buck was taken. A huge nontypical buck scoring 278⅞ was taken by 17-year-old Neil Morin of Falher, Alberta in September of 1991. Morin's record nontypical, taken near Peace River, Alberta, came from considerably farther north than most Alberta hunters expect to find their trophies. This only proves that a monster can occur anywhere in the Wild Rose province. That fact is that many great whitetail bucks are showing up along the Peace River drainage between Fort St. John, British Columbia and the town of Peace River in Alberta.

To put this great buck into perspective, at a final score of 278⅞ net B&C points it is ranked as the fifth largest nontypical on record in the 10th Edition of *Records of North American Big Game,* and it is the *third* largest ever taken by a hunter in all of North America.

Looking back over Alberta's recent whitetail hunting history, these records should come as no surprise. Consider Doug Klinger's 1976 nontypical buck taken from the banks of the Battle River near Hardisty. This 277⅝ monster has numerous large pieces of antler missing, broken off before the deer was shot. I have studied this rack and am convinced that Klinger's buck would have scored well over 300 B&C points, nontypical, had those broken points remained intact. That would have made it one of only three bucks ever to exceed the unbelievable score of 300 inches of nontypical antler.

On November 29, 1984, Jerry Froma shot a huge nontypical buck near his home in Barrhead, Alberta. The buck scored 267⅞ B&C points and currently stands as the Number 11-ranking nontypical whitetail in the 10th Edition of Boone and Crockett's *Records of North American Big Game*.

Also in 1984, on September 25th, bowhunter Dean Dwernychuck arrowed a nontypical buck scoring 241⅛ west of the city of Calgary. Dwernychuck's buck then stood as the Number Three Pope and Young nontypical and was initially ranked as Number 31 in the B&C records. This buck still stands as Canada's largest nontypical whitetail taken with bow and arrow.

In recent months I have been made aware of several other nontypical Alberta monsters which will ultimately fall in among the ranks of the deer I have mentioned above. When all the dust settles, more and more of Alberta's book bucks will continue to compete with one another.

On the typical side, Stephen Jansen's 204⅔ buck, taken in the Dog Pound area northwest of Calgary in 1967, stood for years as Canada's best recorded typical buck. It fell only 1⅞ inches behind the long-standing Jordan Number One typical head. Now eclipsed by the 1993 new world record Hansen buck from Saskatchewan (scoring 213⅜), the Jansen buck is unique in that it possesses more inches of typical antler than any buck ever taken. Unfortunately, uneven lengths of opposing tines resulted in over 20 inches of deductions.

So, given what has transpired in Alberta whitetail hunting in the course of the last 20 years, there is ample reason to expect records to be set and broken. Hopefully this will explain why Alberta continues to appear so regularly in the pages of your favorite hunting magazines.

- Nonresident whitetail hunting success: 60%
- Resident whitetail hunting success: 34%
- 1992 resident whitetail harvest: 25,700 bucks and does combined.
- 1992 nonresident harvest: 780 animals, primarily bucks.
- Current estimated total whitetail population: 250,000.
- 1994 bow season: September 7—October 29.
- 1994 rifle season: October 31—November 26.

Nonresident whitetail license cost: $197.66 Canadian funds.

FOR INFORMATION:

For additional information on seasons and hunting regulations contact:
  Alberta Environmental Protection
  9920 108th St.
  Main Floor
  Information Center
  Edmonton, Alberta
  Canada T5K 2M4
  (403) 422 2079

For a listing of Alberta guides and outfitters, contact:
  Professional Outfitter's Association of Alberta
  15232 84 Avenue
  Edmonton, Alberta
  Canada T5R 3X8
  (403) 486 3050

CHAPTER SIX

SASKATCHEWAN

The sound of an aggressive buck walking through the timber was unmistakable. He made no attempt to be quiet, but rather stopped periodically and battered timber with his antlers. I could not yet see him, but I knew he was a buck.

Two does stood at attention right in front of me. I was 25 feet up in a spruce tree, bow in hand, praying that the buck would come over to visit the does.

Off to my right I could hear him coming ever closer. Then he grunted. The does' eyes were glued to the incoming buck.

I wanted to lift my bow to prepare for the shot, but the does might have caught the movement. I waited. A large spruce bough blocked my view back to the right, in the direction of the approaching buck. It appeared that he would actually step past the bough before I would be able to see him. In other words, at the hopeful moment of first sight I would have to be prepared to shoot. He was coming in from exactly the opposite direction of every other deer I had seen in the three days I'd been hunting this location!

Suddenly the does started walking toward the buck, as if to greet him. When they stepped out of sight under the big spruce bough I lifted my bow and drew. Instantly the buck, a wide eight-pointer, stepped into view and stopped broadside. This was the sixth quality Saskatchewan buck to present me with a broadside shot within bow range in

SASKATCHEWAN

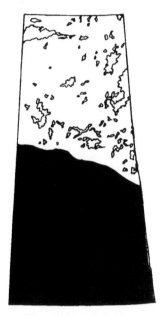

Total Whitetail Range

three consecutive years of hunting the great northern forests of west-central Saskatchewan. I have lost count of how many smaller bucks and does I have had below my stands. They all flow into a stream of deer hunting dreams that continue to lure me back each fall.

Saskatchewan's human population extends approximately half-way up to its northern border. Past this halfway point man's numbers are very limited. The same can be said of the deer population. Let us consider the whitetail-inhabited parts of the province. There are three main divisions: forest, parkland, and grassland. Man has altered most of this landscape and modified with his farming, ranching, and forestry practices.

SASKATCHEWAN

Shaded areas describe where nonresidents may _NOT_ hunt. The forest fringe and forest areas just above the shaded area is where nonresident hunting takes place.

Saskatchewan's deer have benefited from some of this tampering with nature and have even excelled as a result of new land being broken to the plow. There is a critical point that can and has been reached in the southern zones. Tracts of grassland, marsh, and aspen stands that once served as a stronghold for Saskatchewan's whitetail population are disappearing. Some areas have so little cover that even the wiliest of whitetail bucks cannot survive. The alarm button has

SASKATCHEWAN

**Greatest Whitetail
Population Density**

been pushed. Conservation groups are now active in habitat rescue but is it enough or is it too late?

Statistics speak for themselves, and the records show that the once-mighty southern Saskatchewan deer herd has stumbled. Huge bucks are still taken every year "down south," but the consistency is no longer there. You can't blame the deer; it just isn't possible to sneak around in an over-grazed pasture.

The south might not be on track, but the northern parkland and forest fringe areas have been producing more and more trophy heads in recent years. In 1987, the top five typical whitetails recognized by the Saskatchewan Wildlife Federation were taken in the northern parkland/forest

SASKATCHEWAN

**Best Whitetail
Trophy Area**

fringe area. The top nontypical, which scored a whopping 253⅛, was also taken in the forest fringe in the northwestern corner of the province.

What's the reason for this upswing in the northern trophy harvest? The past few winters have been quite easy on Saskatchewan's deer herd and have allowed it to bounce back from the tough winters of '84 and '85. Existing cover is such that many big bucks survive the hunting season in good order and are allowed to pass along their superior genetics. So, at this point there is a healthy population base with good ratios of trophy animals. Also, good buck/doe ratios.

In some areas buck numbers even exceed the number of

As a hunting destination Saskatchewan is attractive for its two-buck limit and legal baiting. Baiting tends to localize does—but where there are does a buck will come 'round sooner or later. (Photo by Judd Cooney)

does. You can imagine what this offers hunters who like to rattle antlers during the rut! The competition among bucks is fierce and they respond aggressively to antler rattling. Add to this the fact that hunters in pursuit of wallhangers are starting to turn their attention to the forest fringe and you have a sound theory for the marked increase in the harvest of huge "northern" racks.

To locate the northern parklands and forest fringe, find a provincial road map. Place your pencil on the western side of the province somewhere around Maidstone. Moving north and eastward, angle up until the line passes through Big River. Now trace all the way across to Carrot River. From here angle south until the point of the pencil rests on Duck Mountain Provincial Park. This, at best, is a rough estimation of the extent of agricultural progress in Saskatchewan. For a detailed look at the forest fringe, maps and aerial photographs are available. Write to the Central Survey and Mapping Agency, Saskatchewan Property Management Corporation, 2nd Floor, 2045 Broad Street, Regina, Saskatchewan, Canada S4P 3T7.

Mature forests produce maximum shade on the forest floor and minimum new growth. Only when the protective closed canopy of the large white and black spruce is opened does revegetation begin. The two most common occurrences that open up forest stands are fire and logging. As shade is removed, the thirst for sunlight is finally abated and the once-dormant seeds begin their race for the sky. This is banquet time for the deer family. One to five years after the canopy is opened the clearing is awash with new, succulent growth. Young saplings, tender shoots, and herbaceous layer all combine to form an attractive food source.

The same situation occurs all along the forest fringe: food bordered by heavy cover. Don't be disappointed if you look over an area such as this without seeing dozens of white flags bounding away. These opened areas are usually quite large and the deer may be scattered all along the boundaries rather than concentrated. You just have to look at it in the sense that quality is more important than quantity.

I love hunting the big northern woods of Saskatchewan. Many people envision Saskatchewan as a flat ocean of grain fields dotted with occasional woodlots, and that's a pretty accurate picture of the southern part of the province. However, as these lines are written nonresidents may not hunt the southern sector of Saskatchewan. To the north (actually about in the middle of the province) nonresidents are still welcome in the vast timberlands and the forest fringe, which thus far have avoided the intrusion of the tractor and plow. This is the land of moose, elk, black bear, timber wolves, and the whitetail deer. The vast mixed forest offers true wilderness hunting, or along the forest fringe you may find alfalfa fields snuggled up against the big woods. Happily, there is an excellent population of whitetails with a buck/doe ratio approaching one to one in many of these areas. For this reason, when conditions are right during the rut, rattling antlers can be very effective.

During November of the 1991 season, while perched in a big spruce tree, I rattled in two wonderful 10-pointers at the same time. One came in about 50 yards from me and never got close enough for a bow shot. The other buck, a shoo-in candidate for Pope and Young, came in from behind me and stood directly below me, shrouded by drooping spruce boughs. I watched him between my feet through the grated floor of my treestand for five heart-pounding minutes before he moved out from under the boughs. As luck would have it he exited the wrong direction for me to get a good shot, so he's still at large somewhere in the vast forests of Saskatchewan. The point is that these bucks will respond to antler rattling!

The deer season opens in mid-September for bow and muzzleloader in the nonresident zone. Hunters may use either arm—and with a two-buck bag limit, you could even use both! Then, come November, the rifle season opens, meaning modern rifles. However, you may still continue with bow or muzzleloader if you wish.

During the bow/muzzleloader season, hunters may wear whatever clothing they desire, meaning all camouflage patterns are legal. However, once the November rifle season opens, regardless of whether you continue to hunt with primitive arms, you must abide by the requirements of a specific dress code. During rifle season, all hunters must wear a *complete* outer suit of solid white, solid blaze orange, solid yellow, or any combination of these three solid

Facing this chapter is Milo Hansen's new world record. This is Saskatchewan's number two typical now, a fabulous 200⅞ buck taken by Peter Swiston in 1983.

colors. Blaze orange camo is illegal. A hat or cap must also be worn, and it can be either yellow or blaze orange, but not white.

Since nonresident hunting is restricted to the great sprawling forests called "Crown Land" by the residents, the natural question is raised, "How do you hunt trophy whitetails systematically in such vast forests?" Admittedly it is something of a needle-in-a-haystack problem, except for the fact that Saskatchewan allows baiting of deer. Without baiting, the odds for success would be so low that there would be no dependable hunting opportunity and nonresident hunting would soon cease to exist for whitetails. The whitetail population in the Crown Forests, being considerably less than in the farmlands, puts the hunter at a marked disadvantage without the assistance of baiting. The two-buck bag limit, plus legal baiting, are the specific reasons many hunters choose Saskatchewan, as opposed to hunts in other prairie provinces.

As these words are hitting the page, there is an emotionally charged movement afoot in Saskatchewan to stop legal baiting. The unfounded cry that baiting is taking ill advantage of the deer and equates hunting over bait to something less than fair chase is substantiated by nothing less than emotional ranting. At present, thanks to several mild winters, the white-tail populations in the Crown Forests of Saskatchewan are at an all-time high, which is reflected by the two-deer bag limit. One bad winter (which is ultimately inevitable) and the whitetail population will plummet and Mother Nature will have to start over building up the herd. For now, however, whitetails exist in above-average numbers.

Tourism stands as one of Saskatchewan's leading industries, and hunters are a big part of that industry. Baiting and a two-buck bag limit are really the key factors that give Saskatchewan the edge over competing provinces.

Hopefully the powers that be in the Saskatchewan government will not be led down the garden path and succumb to wildlife management by unfounded sentiment. Eliminating baiting would end realistic opportunity for nonresidents, who are not allowed to hunt the majority of the province's agricultural lands where, by the way, resident hunters hover around alfalfa and stubble fields waiting for whitetails to step out to . . . you know what. That's right—to feed!

Hunters planning to hunt northern Saskatchewan should monitor this situation closely to be sure what opportunity—or lack thereof—awaits them.

Hunters can expect a wide range of hunting conditions, depending on the week and month they choose to hunt. In September the weather can be very mild, even on the

Here's a fabulous Saskatchewan eight-pointer taken by outfitter Paul Marek during the early archery/muzzleloader season near Chitek Lake. (Photo by David Kelbert)

warm side. Then, after mid-October, snow can come at any time. During my 1992 hunt, in the third week of October, we experienced snow and temperatures a bit below freezing on the low end. By the end of that week the snow had melted and the skies were clear with temperatures reaching a high in the 50's. Come November, it's always wise to expect real cold and snow.

On my first hunt with Caribou Trail Outfitters in 1990, in the northern forests, I hunted the last two weeks of November and endured temperatures as cold as 30 degrees below zero! I remember wondering what would happen if I drew my bow in that extreme cold. I envisioned coming to full draw and having to wait until spring thaw for the bow to shoot! That wasn't quite the case; I arrowed two beautiful

Guide Danny Halko displays a lovely 14-point Boone and Crockett typical taken by one of his nonresident hunters along the forest fringe. (Photo by David Kelbert)

10-pointers in spite of the cold. There is no question that cold weather spells better hunting in the far north. Thirty below zero doesn't phase a Saskatchewan whitetail. It won't phase a hunter, either—if he's dressed right.

The two-buck limit applies to most zones a nonresident may hunt. Even if the outfitter charges a trophy fee on the second deer, it will still be the cheapest Canadian deer hunt you can buy. Alberta to the west and Manitoba to the east offer a one-whitetail limit, making Saskatchewan's two-deer limit extremely attractive to nonresidents. In zones with a two-deer limit the tags can be purchased one at a time or both at the same time. It's up to the hunter. Nonresidents are required to hire a licensed guide, so do-it-yourself hunting is taboo.

Brian Stein took Saskatchewan's best archery nontypical. This buck is actually barely a nontypical with lovely double drop points! (Photo by Brian Stein)

Choosing the right rifle and caliber for Saskatchewan deer depends on the terrain you're going to be hunting. A .30-30 might be ideal if you're hunting from a treestand in tight timber—but a .270 or 7mm magnum might be more suitable if you're hunting more open terrain or watching long cutlines in the timber. Outfitter Paul Marek recommends that rifles of .30 caliber and larger be considered. Marek says, "It is common for our hunters to see large bucks in tight brush. In the event of bullet deflection on twigs or saplings, the heavier calibers seem to carry through where the zippier, lighter bullets fail and sometimes wound deer. It's not that it takes so much more power to bring down a big buck, it's just extra insurance in thick-timber situations."

Paul Marek and partner Dave Kelbert, proprietors of Caribou Trail Outfitters, are both avid blackpowder hunters. They prefer and recommend large bores no less than .50

caliber, firing heavy conical hollowpoint bullets of 350 grains or more. A 300-pound whitetail is not unusual in Saskatchewan, so the added knockdown power is a good idea. The exit wound is critical since much of the muzzle-loader season occurs before the snow flies. A good blood trail from a bullet exit is very critical on dry ground and in thick timber. Saskatchewan does not discriminate against the modern muzzleloader, and any type caplock or flintlock rifle is legal. Scopes on muzzleloaders are legal as well.

There is also a shotgun season in proximity to some of the larger cities. These seasons are in the residents-only zones, so are not of importance to nonresident hunters. Handguns, of course, are illegal, as they are across Canada.

The price of whitetail hunts available in Saskatchewan varies a great deal. You may find hunts as low as $1000 or as high as $3000 and more. Experience has taught me you get what you pay for. There are some good, experienced outfitters in the province—as well as some who operate on a shoestring and understand little about the game they hunt. It's really up to the hunter to determine which is which, so do your homework carefully. Considering the cost of the hunt, the travel, the license, etc., the cheapest but most critical part of the investment should always be phone calls to legitimate hunter references. If an outfitter cannot provide enough hunter references to convince you that he's really producing good bucks for his clients on an ongoing basis, you'd be a fool to book a hunt with him. And don't be bamboozled by the fact that one of his hunters shot a huge book deer. In Saskatchewan that can happen to the least able outfitter. What really counts is the rule, not the exception.

My philosophy about hunting the megabucks of western Canada is that you should view it as a three-year plan. If you can only afford to go once in your life, you might be

Saskatchewan's best archery typical buck is a real monster that took a lot of deductions for its 166⅝ score. Robert Temple arrowed it in 1985. (Photo by Robert Temple)

setting yourself up for disappointment. Even in the best camp, weather conditions can deal you a bad hand and you may come home without a buck. Even with all the factors going right, it is possible to just be in the wrong place at the wrong time.

It happened to me last season on my Saskatchewan hunt. It seemed that no matter what stand I chose, the bucks were somewhere else. The other hunters in camp were seeing scads of bucks and getting shots daily while I twiddled my thumbs and watched the grass grow. Four out of five hunters would tell you that it was the most unbelievable hunt they had ever been on. I would have called it slow, if I didn't know what the other hunters were experiencing. But that's what I mean about investing yourself in a three-year plan. Given that you've made all the right choices in terms of the outfitter, you still have to be lucky. That's just hunting.

Elburn Kottler's huge nontypical, taken in 1957, scored a whopping 265⅜. The rack alone weighed 11½ pounds! (Photo by Elburn Kottler)

My luck finally did turn around on that last day of my 1992 hunt, as described at the beginning of this article. The buck stopped broadside and I slipped an XX78 behind his shoulder. He hopped forward and looked around, unsure of what had stung him. Within seconds his rear end began to sway and sag, and then he tipped over, not 20 yards from my treestand.

I will hunt whitetails in Saskatchewan again this season. It's in my blood. I really believe that if I stick with it, I'll take one of those great forest giants with my bow. I'm not talking about a Pope and Young buck. I'm referring to a big B&C critter, so big it takes two dogs to bark at him. Someone in our Saskatchewan camp gets one every year. My number is coming up one of these days.

- Nonresident whitetail hunting success averages from 65 to 70%.
- Resident whitetail hunting success averages 75 to 80%.
- Total 1993 whitetail harvest (resident and nonresident combined): 45,000
- Five bucks were harvested for each doe.
- Best deer-producing area: Parkland/forest fringe regions.
- 1994 bow season: August 29—October 29.
- 1994 rifle season: October 31—December 3.
- Nonresident whitetail license: $291 each, Canadian funds.

FOR INFORMATION:

For additional regulatory information, contact:
    Saskatchewan Environment and Resource Management
    3211 Albert Street
    Regina, Saskatchewan
    Canada S4S 5W6
    (306) 787 2700

For listings of guides and outfitters, contact:
    Tourism Saskatchewan
    Saskatchewan Trade and Environment Center
    1919 Saskatchewan Dr.
    Regina, Saskatchewan
    Canada S4P 3V7
    (800) 667 7191

CHAPTER SEVEN

MANITOBA

Manitoba offers a wide variety of differing whitetail habitat. The western edge from Virden south, noted for bluff hunting, has high numbers, but due to habitat loss and hunting pressure the bucks barely survive into their third year. Although the occasional buck survives long enough to develop impressive antlers, the growing tendency for the area is toward smaller racks.

As one moves farther east, there is a gradual transition to a more hilly type of terrain. This is prevalent in areas such as the Pembina Hills, Brandon Hills, and the highly productive Spruce Woods Provincial Park. These areas, which have more dense tree cover and fewer people, offer a great whitetail refuge. This makes it harder on the hunters—and conversely easier for the deer.

Moving yet farther east, you move from the rolling land of the Pembina Hills into the top-rate Manitoba farmland of the Red River Valley. This land, for lack of a more descriptive term, is flat. So flat, in fact, that when covered with winter snow it resembles an endless frozen lake. Although there is a very high human population base with minimal whitetail cover, the Red and Assiniboine Rivers and their tributaries provide sufficient cover to boast a good whitetail population. Because of the high degree of agricultural activity the game unit north of Winnipeg and

Manitoba's current record bucks are, left, Ben Delaronde's 258⅛ non-typical and, right, Larry McDonald's 197⅞ typical. (Photo by Randy Bean)

the unit south of the city to the U.S. border have been restricted to bowhunting only.

Again, heading farther east, one gradually moves away from farmland into the Sandiland area, and onto the leading edge of the Pre-Cambrian Shield. Throughout the area the sand ridges and swales produce a scattered mix of deciduous and coniferous trees, with a gradual transition to mainly coniferous in the Whiteshell Park. In the far southeastern portion of the province, bordering Ontario, the swampy black spruce areas take over. These areas all support a healthy whitetail population, but, as there are fewer roads, this area is more difficult to hunt than the agricultural areas.

North of the Virden area the rolling farmland leads into the large hills of the Duck and Porcupine Mountain ranges,

MANITOBA

Total Whitetail Range

sandwiched between the Saskatchewan border and Lake Winnipegosis. Although not resembling mountains in the normal sense, the huge rolling hills offer a very scenic hunt with a good deer population.

East of the Manitoba mountains, the Interlake area is bordered on the west by Lake Winnipeg and on the east by Lake Manitoba. This area has few roads traveling through it and has a high deciduous tree cover with scattered evergreens, and is laced with bands of swamps and meadows. It would be rated as difficult to hunt, but rates high as a probable area to produce that once-in-a-lifetime buck.

When it comes to choosing a firearm for Manitoba whitetail, the terrain in which you're hunting will usually

MANITOBA

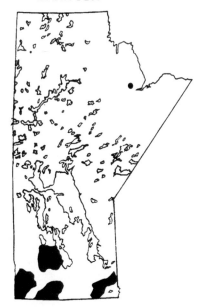

**Greatest Whitetail
Population Density**

be a determining factor. For the more heavily wooded ravines, the ever-popular .30-30 will be more than adequate. A faster caliber up into the .308 range will be a sensible minimum when hunting the more open terrain. With some shots at 150 to 200 yards, high speed and high impact are essential. At these ranges and beyond hotter calibers in the right hands are very effective.

Hunting methods utilized throughout the province are as varied as the terrain itself. For hunting the bluffs, the push and post method is common and effective. Two or three hunters will stand or post along the end of a rectangular patch of brush, usually some 200 yards wide by a

MANITOBA

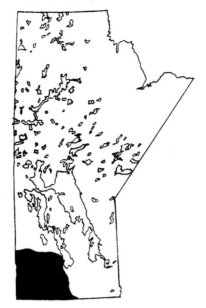

**Best Whitetail
Trophy Area**

quarter-mile long. Their hunting partners then start in at the other end, pushing the deer onto the posters. It is not uncommon to have a dozen deer explode from the bush within yards of the posters. Being situated in agricultural land, it is also not uncommon to have one of Mr. Brown's cows break out of the cover as well. For this reason extreme care must be exercised when using this method.

In hunting the hilly country and ravines that run between the ridges, a pusher is normally relegated to moving along the bottom of the ravine, driving the deer up and onto his hunting partners who are moving along the ridges above. From a vantage point on the ridges, one can either

The provincial typical record for bowhunters is Lloyd Lintott's beautiful 181⅙ buck. (Photo by Randy Bean)

Ted Hryhoruk arrowed the provincial nontypical Pope and Young record, a buck scoring 202⅜. (Photo by Randy Bean)

take a shot or shout over to a partner that a deer is on its way up. These ravines also give the lone hunter the opportunity to slowly move along the edges of the rim, either stalking a spotted deer or moving into position ahead of the animal. The ravines, which can be as short as a couple hundred yards—or run for several miles—are blanketed with oak and poplar, thick hazelnut underbrush, and usually have thick willow beds in the lower wetland areas. The highlands between ravines are generally cultivated farmland, making crops a very effective lure. One thing common to the most productive hunting areas throughout the province is the close relationship to agrculture.

If there's any amount of bush or a wooded ravine running adjacent to a farmer's field, you can rest assured there'll be deer close at hand. Being in such close proximity to cultivation, the whitetails' food source, from spring to fall, is directly linked to farm crops. The deer become so dependent, in fact, that many farmers make annual application to the Crop Insurance Corporation for compensation for crop loss. The fresh, green shoots of cereal grains or a field full of alfalfa will draw deer for miles.

Surprisingly enough, a real favorite are the immature heads of the sunflower plant. The towering stalks of this plant, as well as corn, actually take over as main bedding areas, with herds of 20 or more deer spending the entire summer within the crops. Once the fall harvest starts, the deer shift into the unharvested portion, with combines passing within yards of the deer. As the firearm season starts well after harvest, only the bowhunters can take full advantage of these feeding and bedding habits.

Although the firearm hunters have higher success rates, bowhunting continues to build in popularity in Manitoba. Bowhunters must adhere to the same general rules that pertain to gun hunters, but are exempt from the blaze orange dress requirements. Archers may make full use of camouflage in the bow-only season. All bowhunters must use a longbow or recurve requiring no less than 40 pounds draw weight at 28-inch draw. Compound bows must be set

Gene Race of Winnipeg and his hunting partners found these three Manitoba bucks locked together, one of few known cases of three bucks being locked up. (Photo by Glenn Olsen)

Here's a nice typical Canadian buck scoring in the 140's. Many Canadian bucks reach this antler size at an early age. (Photo by Randy Bean)

at peak draw weight of no less than 40 pounds. Broadheads must be no less than 7/8-inch wide, and it goes without saying that it is illegal to be in possession of any other arm or contrivance that may be used to take game during the bow season.

With the large area south of Winnipeg restricted to archery hunting, a large number of bowhunters carry out their hunting here. Being in such close proximity to such a high human population, one would wonder at the bowhunting success rate. However, several hunters I know

Canadian whitetails don't have to make B&C to be extremely impressive. This fine Manitoba buck taken by Jack Brown nets just under 160. (Photo by Randy Bean)

Ken Warkentin took this 177⅝ typical B&C buck in 1987 near San-ford, Manitoba. This is a classic example of a Canadian buck that would be easy to underestimate. (Photo by Randy Bean)

have taken deer in the past eight consecutive seasons just a half-hour drive from Winnipeg. Bowhunters have it hands-down over the rifle hunters when it comes to length of sea-son and the quality of weather in which to hunt. The season runs from the last week in August to the middle of November in the majority of the province, extending to the end of November in the restricted bowhunting-only area.

The archery zone is divided by the Red River, with a se-ries of tibutaries running into the main stream. The mean-dering creeks and rivers form a series of loops fully treed with scrub oak and poplar, with thick willow beds in pock-ets throughout the area. As these streams are bordered on both sides by agricultural land, it offers the deer ample cover and excellent forage. As farm crops are eventually harvested, the deer revert back to normal feeding patterns. Other than the occasional feed of alfalfa, which remains edible until first frost, the deer feed on a mix of grasses, buds, wild clover, and acorns, thanks to the abundance of oaks in the area.

The advent of the killing frost signals the start of the rut. This corresponds nicely with both the firearms and archery season, peaking in the last two weeks of November. As the bow season isn't as hectic as the rifle season, the rut plays right into the bowhunters' hands. The meandering streams and the cover they provide set up a convenient runway for amorous bucks, with some of the more dominant ones servicing a three to four-mile stretch—with several scrapes along the way. To effectively hunt a scrape, it's almost essential that one hunt from the time-proven treestand.

Although a number of deer are taken from the ground, the treestand continually proves to be the popular and sensible choice. A well-elevated stand, with the proper choice of camouflage, will give you your best chances. With the bow season running for over three months, the serious bowhunter really has to dress for the season. In late August, when the trees are still fully in leaf, the standard leaf pattern works well. This will change to fall colors, to bare gray trees, and then to the white patterns most effective when the ground is blanketed by a foot of snow. You'll also go from hunting in a camo T-shirt in 80-degree weather to an insulated suit in a shivering 30 below zero.

Due to the high agricultural influence, the majority of prime hunting lands in the southern portion of the province are privately owned by local farmers. It is illegal to hunt on any private land without the landowner's permission. This applies whether or not the land is posted. Private land ownership maps are available from the municipal offices, obtained by calling Repro Map in Dauphin, Manitoba at (204) 638 3584 or 638 5058, or by calling the municipal office in the town nearest your point of interest.

Those hunting areas that fall in Wildlife Management

Areas and Provincial Parks, referred to as Crown Land, may be hunted without permission, so be certain you know where you're hunting. Crown Land maps are available by telephoning (204) 945 6666.

Anyone hunting whitetails within Manitoba must be in possession of a valid hunting license. Deer licenses are readily and equally available to residents and nonresidents alike. Nonresident non-Canadians must be accompanied by a licensed Manitoba guide, and no more than two hunters may utilize the services of a guide simultaneously.

With the province continually producing large world-class bucks, there are a goodly number of nonresidents who put Manitoba on their hunting calendars year after year. The higher license fee and guide requirement for non-Canadians are the only additional restriction placed on nonresidents.

The Provincial Wildlife Department keeps close tabs on the licensed guides to insure nonresidents are guaranteed the services of reputable and competent guides. With relatively few nonresidents taking out licenses, "outsiders" are typically well-received and enjoy quality whitetail hunting. There are just a dozen outfitters, listed in the *Manitoba Lodges and Outfitters Guide,* who include deer hunts as part of their services. A free copy of this guide may be obtained by phoning (204) 889 2840. Although there is no additional charge levied for trophy heads, tags issued with the hunting license must be affixed to all meat, antlers, and hides to be exported prior to transportation or export.

With the high degree of wildlife management being exercised by the Provincial Wildlife Branch, the whitetail population is in good shape. The greatest detriment to deer survival in Manitoba is harsh winters. Extreme cold, combined with heavy snowfall, make it difficult for the deer to find food. Expending more energy digging for food than

Randy Bean rattled up and arrowed this lovely 168⅜ Manitoba typical in 1992. (Photo by Randy Bean)

they receive from what they uncover, deer can die a horrible death in a tough winter. The private wildlife associations play a vital role in assisting provincial wildlife officials in deer feeding projects in areas that experience excessive snowfall. Feeding starving deer is a tricky business, but with good cooperation between these two groups, Manitoba's feeding programs have become very successful.

Luckily, Manitoba has enjoyed milder winters with moderate snowfall for the past several years; this has left the deer population in good shape at this writing. The province has an estimated whitetail population of over 100,000, with a steady increase over the past several years.

Overall, resident firearms hunters enjoy a whopping 70 percent success rate on whitetails. Nonresident firearms hunters, being more trophy-conscious, still average a 50 percent success rate. Even the bowhunters in Manitoba enjoy a 30 percent success rate, higher than the firearms success rate in many parts of the United States. Not only are these success rates unusually high by comparative North American hunter success, but Manitoba enjoys the lowest hunter per capita rate in North America!

According to the 1992 edition of the Manitoba Big Game Association's record book, the number one typical whitetail, scoring 195⅞, was taken by George Harris in 1988. The number two typical spot goes to Eric Murray with his 194⅝ buck taken in 1991.

The best Manitoba nontypical goes to Ken Hawkins with his 256⅝-inch buck taken in 1973. The number two nontypical, scoring 242, was taken by Murray Strachan in 1979.

At the time of this writing I am advised that two monster whitetails were taken by Manitoba native Indian hunters just before the regular 1994 bow season opened. One typical five by five buck, still in velvet, scored 190; a 30-point nontypical, also in velvet, scored 240. That's quite a start for 1994! Native Indians are not governed by regulated hunting seasons.

Facts and figures are all nice, but what everyone wants is a map with an "X" marking the spot for the next Manitoba record. If I were a betting man (along with a little inside information), I'd put my money on the Spruce Woods/Brandon Hills region, and in the North Interlake in the vicinity of Mulvihill, Fisher Branch, or the Sleeve Lake area. Although these would probably be your best spots, all areas of the province produce big bucks. One just may have your name on him!

- Total number of rifle hunters, 1993 season: 36,000.
- Resident success rate: 70 percent.
- Nonresident success rate: 50 percent.
- Total resident and nonresident bowhunters in 1993: 3500.
- Combined bowhunter success rate: 30 percent.
- Resident whitetail license cost, 1994: $25 Canadian funds.
- Nonresident whitetail license cost, 1994: $176.50 Canadian funds.
- Top three whitetail producing areas in 1993:
  1. Spruce Woods.
  2. Interlake area.
  3. Riding Mountain area.

FOR INFORMATION:

For Manitoba whitetail hunting seasons and information, contact:

Manitoba Natural Resources
Box 22,
1495 James Street
Winnipeg, Manitoba
Canada R3H 0W9
(204) 945 6784

For a listing of Manitoba guides and outfitters, contact:

Travel Manitoba
Dept. AF-4
7th Floor, 155 Carlton Street
Winnipeg, Manitoba
Canada R3C3H8
(204) 945 3777l

CHAPTER EIGHT

THE COLD, HARD FACTS ABOUT CANADIAN WHITETAIL HUNTING

I was telling a friend in Dallas, Texas about my incredibly lucky bowhunt in Saskatchewan last November and the question finally came up: "How cold does it get up there?"

"Oh, anywhere from freezing to 30 below," I answered.

"How long do you stay in your treestand?"

"From before daylight 'til dark, unless I arrow a buck," I replied.

He looked at me like I had two heads. "I don't know how you do it . . . I'd freeze my buns off before I'd been there an hour," he said, shrugging his shoulders and shivering.

His conclusion was typical of hunters who aren't used to hunting in cold weather or, better put, haven't mastered cold weather hunting. Lots of people hunt in the cold, but in truth, most of them cave in and retreat for the tropics. I don't deserve a medal for staying in my treestand at 20 or 30 below for eight or nine hours. Psychiatric examination, perhaps, but no medals. You can bet I'm comfortable or I wouldn't be there. If I deserve any credit at all, it's for 25 years of researching a means of staying comfortable in temperatures that typically terrorize the imaginations of thin-blooded deer hunters.

Dressing right makes the difference between success and failure in freezing cold. Dressing for the cold is a science that dramatically increases ones odds for success, not to mention enjoyment of the hunt. (Photy by Judd Cooney)

Seldom a day goes by that I don't get a call from someone thinking about heading to western Canada for a November deer hunt. Along with the usual questions about outfitters, terrain, best rifle calibers or archery tackle, I ultimately find myself in an in-depth telephone seminar about how to survive the cold. After all, that's often the difference between hunter success and failure.

I lived in Alberta, Canada, for 22 years and 18 of those were spent outfitting hunters. I knew that in order for my hunters to be successful, especially my November whitetail hunters, my greatest challenge was keeping them in stands as long as possible. Early in the game it became quite clear that they could seldom find the "right stuff" in their home

The Chimo Boot is a Canadian boot originally designed for Canadian Forces on Arctic maneuvers. Its unique mukluk design is perfect for deer hunters in snow and cold.

states to keep them warm. What would a Texas, Alabama, or Florida hunter know about staying in a treestand all day at 30 below zero? The answer to that question is "NOTHING!"

So now, as if you had just called me on the phone and asked how you're going to survive a November whitetail hunt in western Canada, I'm going to tell you exactly how it's done. I'll be dealing specifically with hunters who will be taking a stand and sitting for long periods of time with limited movement, as is typical of blind and treestand hunters. If you follow my advice *exactly*, you will stay warm no matter how cold the weather you face. The system I am about to describe has been tested in temperatures down to 85 degrees below zero without casualties. Pay close attention to detail here and you'll be prepared for whatever Mother Nature throws at you.

Warm Feet

Let's start at the bottom and work our way up. Most hunters throw in the towel as soon as their feet cave in to the cold. I have tried every boot known to mankind and the *only one* that withstands subzero temperatures while sitting for long hours is the Chimo Boot. This boot was originally manufactured exclusively for the Canadian Armed Forces for their Arctic maneuvers.

The Chimo Boot is a large, soft, and floppy boot which leaves something to be desired for long-distance walking but for sitting it has no equal. The boot consists of several removable components including a vulcanized nylon outer shell cleated with a soft rubber sole. Inside the shell is a double-layered wool duffel sock which is the main key to keeping feet warm. Pure wool retains 90 percent of its insulative value even when wet. Most felt-pac boots have a felt liner which guarantees frozen feet when the felt becomes damp with perspiration. The wool duffel sock in the Chimo Boot has this problem solved. Under the duffel sock is a felt insole and beneath the insole is a plastic mesh frost trap which collects any moisture forming in the boot and pulls it away from the foot. The boot laces loosely around

The components of the Chimo Boot are: outer shell, double wool felt liner, felt insole, and mesh frost trap.

the foot and lower leg in a mukluk fashion and creates no pressure points which may impair circulation.

The Chimo Boot sells for about $250 Canadian and can be purchased from Totem Outdoor Outfitters, 7430-99 Street, Edmonton, Alberta, Canada T6E 3R9, (403) 432 1223. They are available in white or Navy blue. Totem out-

Ice Breaker Boot Blankets worn over hunting boots while on a stand combat even the most ferocious subzero temperatures.

fitters advises hunters to order early to avoid the last-minute shortages which often occur in the fall.

I've spent hours sitting in sub-freezing weather with no discomfort thanks to Chimo Boots. There are other boots that look similar, but there is just one Chimo Boot. Beware of felt liners in other boots of similar design. They don't compare.

Chimo Boots are the best cold weather stand-hunting boots made as far as I'm concerned. However, I am quick to point out that weather can actually get too cold for them. When temperatures drop to minus 20 degrees and lower, it's time to add another component to your Chimo Boots. Soft, insulated boot overshells called Icebreaker Boot Blankets are the key. Boot Blankets slide over your Chimo Boots and zip up at the rear. When Boot Blankets are worn over Chimo Boots, there's no weather cold enough to freeze you out. The Icebreaker Boot Blankets are available from quality sporting goods stores and sportsmen's mail order houses such as Bass Pro Shops for about $50 per pair. For more information about Boot Blankets and Hand Blankets, contact Icebreaker, Inc., P.O. Box N, Clarksville, GA 30523, phone (706) 754 3732.

The bottoms of Boot Blankets are covered with Cordura, a hard-wearing water-resistant nylon fabric. The only problem with it is that it's noisy. That's not good for bowhunters in treestands. When you slide your foot over the metal grate of a treestand platform, Cordura will make too much noise. Even if you accidentally rub one foot against another, Cordura rubbing against Cordura could make enough noise to attract a deer's attention. So, here's the answer from Raven Wear of Canada. It's a Boot Blanket Cover which is actually a polar fleece oversock which slips on over your Boot Blanket and is tied with a drawstring at the top.

The Raven Wear Boot Blanket Covers completely silence

Raven Wear's soft polar fleece over booties will fit right over the Ice Breaker Boot Blankets, adding extra insulation and keeping the Cordura Boot Blankets quiet for close-range bowhunting.

your Boot Blankets and actually add yet another degree of warmth. Boot Blanket Covers cost $30 U.S. and can be ordered from Raven Wear of Canada, Box 411, Caroline, Alberta, Canada T0M 0M0, phone (403) 722 3896. For $40 you can buy your Boot Blanket Covers with sherpa (imitation sheep fleece) lining.

With Chimo Boots you don't wear heavy socks. I wear a thin synthetic fiber sock to wick moisture away from my foot. Over that I wear a typical wool hunting sock. With the Chimo Boot it is imperative that you do not wear so many heavy socks that your foot fits tight in the boot. A loose fit is the key to warmth. A tight fit restricts circulation and freeze-out is the quick result.

By now you may be saying, "Three different garments just for my feet?"

The new LaCrosse Ice King is an American-made boot that rivals the Chimo Boot for cold weather comfort. It's a good choice if walking is involved.

So I answer your question with one of my own: "Why would a sane hunter spend $3000 or more for a Canadian deer hunt, and then ignore the best advice he'll ever get on how to keep from freezing his feet? Do you want that buck on your wall or not?"

If your style of hunting will require extensive walking as well as some sitting, LaCrosse Footwear has answered the call with the introduction of their Ice King Pac Boot, the warmest, most comfortable pac boot available. Triple-insulated, the Ice King features a double-insulated outer boot plus a thick foam and felt liner that provides extraordinary comfort and unsurpassed warmth in temperatures exceeding −85 degrees.

The upper is constructed of 1000 denier Coran® fabric. Known for its flexibility and resistance to abrasion, Coran ensures comfort, durability, and water resistance. Triple-lock stitching of the Coran top and distressed leather trim to the rubber bottom enhances durability and good looks.

The boot's ozone-resistant rubber bottom is constructed with B-400 Thinsulate, providing a lightweight layer of dry warmth. For maximum insulation value, the Thinsulate is combined with ¼-inch Omalon open-cell foam.

A rugged tractor-tread outsole provides sure-footed traction. A ½-inch felt midsole locks out cold from below. The removable ½-inch open-cell, quick-drying foam and 9mm wool felt liner cushions the foot while resisting moisture and compression, ensuring full insulating capabilities.

Added comfort is provided by the Ice King's thermoplastic heel counter which prevents heel slippage, and a fiberglass shank which provides sturdy support.

The ideal boot for cold climates, the Ice King is superb for those who have difficulty keeping their feet warm in cold weather. It's also ideal for cold-weather construction work, hunting, or stationary sporting activities such as snowmobiling, ice fishing, or dogsledding. Size availability is men's 6–15. More information on the Ice King is available from LaCrosse Footwear, Inc., PO Box 1328, LaCrosse, WI 54602. Suggested retail is $135.00.

Underwear

For the hunter who will be sitting motionless for long hours in extreme cold, I recommend the Patagonia Expedition Weight Capilene Underwear tops and bottoms. The expedition weight underwear is a velour-like fabric with brushed inner and outer surfaces for loft and comfort, and it also wicks perspiration or condensation away from the body. Patagonia's Expedition Weight Capilene Underwear can be purchased at most quality backpacking-oriented mountain shops or directly from Patagonia Mail Order, Inc., P.O. Box 8900, Bozeman, MT 59715, phone (406) 587 7771. Bottoms currently list for $45; tops for $59 (Zip-T neck) or $55 (Wallace Beery button-up neck).

Raven Wear Anti-freeze System

This special multi-component system is ideal for extreme cold weather hunting. The Anti-Freeze system for bow-hunters includes a popular three-quarter length unlined hooded jacket, a watch cap, a sherpa-lined vest, and sherpa-lined bib overalls. The rifle hunter is less concerned with arm mobility since shouldering a rifle is less demanding on the arms than drawing a bow. For this reason the rifle hunter may prefer the Anti-Freeze system with sherpa-lined overalls and fully sherpa-lined coat. The lined coat would replace the vest and unlined jacket.

All are made of 100 percent Dacron Polyester Fleece (polar fleece). This fabric is extremely soft and quiet and

Patagonia's Expedition Weight Capilene Underwear is tops as an inner layer for bitter weather whitetail hunting, especially when sitting still for prolonged periods.

offers easy care and rapid drying. It absorbs no more than one percent of its weight in water, making it useful in showery conditions. The sherpa lining resembles lamb's wool and is also 100 percent polyester. Because of its loft, it allows air to be trapped and when combined with fleece offers maximum warmth for use in extreme cold conditions. The warmth to weight ratio is very high, making this system an ideal choice for cold weather hunting. The same system also works well in moderate conditions where dampness is a chilling factor. Fleece garments, experts agree, perform best when used in combination with hydrophobic underwear such as the Patagonia long johns mentioned earlier.

The sherpa-lined overalls and vest or jacket offer a double covering of the critical kidney area of the lower torso. The kidney region requires extra warmth for added staying power. The Raven Wear system accommodates this need by design! Another handy feature is a knee-high zipper on the overall legs which allows them to slip on over boots.

I wear the Anti-Freeze system over Patagonia long underwear with a light sweater and I'm set for the harshest conditions.

Whether used all together or in part, the Anti-Freeze system is ideal for a wide range of hunting conditions. It is available in Real Tree All Purpose, TreBark, TreBark Universal, and Blaze Orange camo, all with black sherpa; or in solid white fleece with white sherpa. The Anti-Freeze system (bowhunter's version including bib overalls, vest, unlined jacket, and watch cap) sells for $280 U.S. The bib overalls with fully sherpa-lined jacked and watch cap sells for $231.50 U.S.

Raven Wear makes yet another cold-fighting garment which is ideal for hunters who plan to hunt from ground blinds or other ground locations. It's called the Stand Bag,

Raven Wear's Anti-Freeze System is soft, quiet, and warm even in the coldest deer hunting weather. It's made in two models, one for bowhunters and one for riflemen.

and is essentially a beefed-up version of the European hunting bag. The Stand Bag is constructed with a synthetic hollow fiber fill lining, doubled over the foot area, and covered with a heavy wool duffel outer shell. The combination of synthetic and wool insulation offers exceptional warmth and comfort in a wool-quiet garment, ideal when the temperature plunges to 30 below zero! The stand bag features a heavy-duty three-quarter-length zipper on the side, making for easy entry. A large fleece-lined hand muff is sewn onto the front of the Stand Bag making other hand-warming devices unnecessary. A drawstring draws the bag snug around the upper body to keep cold air out. Suspenders hold the Stand Bag at mid-chest level while sitting or standing.

Back in my Alberta hunting days I asked Susan Hindbo of Raven Wear to make a prototype of the Stand Bag for use during the whitetail season. I had located a large scrape that was being frequented by a good buck in the corner of a pasture in very low brush. There were no trees anywhere near the area in which to hide a hunter for an ambush. The only place that offered a vantage point overlooking the scrape was nearly 200 yards away on the top of a rise in the middle of a plowed field. There was a foot of snow on the ground so I laid a white tarp on the snow and had my hunter put on the Stand Bag and lie down on the tarp. Then I folded the white tarp over him, leaving him nearly invisible in the snow.

The temperature was 22 below zero. I told the hunter to stay there until dark, when I'd return to fetch him. He was from Louisiana and the thought of lying in the snow for three hours in that temperature terrified him. I assured him he'd be safe. When I returned at dark he was lying there sound asleep in his Stand Bag, as comfortable as he could be!

The Ice Breaker Hand Blanket is ideal for protecting the rifle hunter's hands in bitter cold. Woolie Boogers, individual fleece hand warmers, are handier for bowhunters because they hang at the hip instead of in your lap.

The Stand Bag eliminates the need for heavily insulated pants and special boots. From the bottoms of your feet up to your mid-chest you're insulated to the max. All you require in addition is a parka and a warm hat. The Raven Wear Stand Bag sells for $300 U.S. and doubles as a handy stadium bag for sports events or as an emergency blanket for autombile travel.

Hand Warmers

There has never been a glove or mitten in existence which will keep hands warm all day while sitting motionless in subzero weather. Save your time and energy and take my word for it . . . they don't exist! What does exist are hand-muffs which will do what gloves and mittens won't. My pick of the commercial handmuffs, especially for industrial grade cold weather, is the Ice Break Hand Blanket, made by the same folks who make the Boot Blankets mentioned earlier.

Jam both hands into the Hand Blanket and the results are simply amazing. Hands stay warm hour after hour, even in severe cold. I don't wear any gloves at all, even in the coldest conditions. Gloves actually restrict circulation and work against you in the long run. A *caveat* to that is, in extremely cold weather, gun hunters should wear something like a silk or polypropolene glove liner; you must not touch metal in extreme cold, and that includes a rifle bolt.

The only way you can improve on the Hand Blanket is to use a dry chemical handwarmer inside—and there's a zippered compartment to hold a supply of chemical warmers.

The Hand Blanket features a waist tie which enables the user to wear the warmer around his or her waist so it stays put when you need both hands for shooting. Available in a

Raven Wear offers these Anti-Freeze System Handsavers, individual insulated pouches which hang at the hip, ideal for bowhunters.

variety of camo patterns, the Hand Blankets retail for about $25. A good source is Bass Pro Shops.

Bowhunters may prefer the Woolie Boogers offered by Screaming Eagle or the Anti-Freeze Hand Savers made by

Raven Wear of Canada. Woolie Boogers are individual hand pouches made of sheepskin with the leather side out and the wool fleece on the inside. They can be looped onto your belt, one on each hip, so when it's time for the shot both hands can be used and the Woolie Boogers hang at the hip, out of the way of the bowstring. Screaming Eagle, Inc. (P.O. Box 4507, Missoula, MT 59806, phone 1-(800)-458 2017) sells them for about $50 per pair.

Raven Wear's Anti-Freeze Hand Savers accomplish the same task but for less money. Hand Savers also clip to the user's belt for handy hip location. They are made of 100 percent gray wool duffel with sherpa lining for extra warmth. Knit cuffs fit snugly around the wrists to eliminate heat loss. Raven Wear sells their Hand Savers for $30 U.S. per pair.

Both Woolie Boogers and Hand Savers will keep hands warm down to freezing or a bit below, and for colder weather I recommend their use in conjunction with chemical handwarmers.

Although I usually shoot barehanded when I'm rifle hunting, I recommend taking along a thick pair of wool, synthetic, or soft leather gloves for the reason mentioned above—and also to wear when climbing into your treestand. Those treesteps are burning cold to the bare hand in subzero weather. Bowhunters will also benefit from a thin pair of gloves for gripping their bow handles. Bow handles get pretty frosty, too! I like to shoot my bow barehanded, so I cover the grip with polypropylene fabric, fleece side out. This enables me to hold the bow handle indefinitely, even barehanded.

Beware of trying to shoot a rifle with bulky gloves. On several occasions I have seen accidental discharges occur when hunters wore thick, bulky gloves. The problem is that you can't feel the trigger through all that bulk. The trigger

These components make a perfect threesome for protecting the head, face, and neck in extreme cold.

finger actually touches the trigger, but you don't know it until the rifle fires. Be smart—keep your hands in your handwarmer for warmth, then shoot either barehanded or with very thin gloves so you can feel the trigger properly.

Head, Neck and Face Warmers

It's critical to protect your hands and head in cold weather. These are the two primary areas where heat loss occurs. If you have a Raven Wear Anti-Freeze system you already have a polar fleece watch cap which is soft and very warm, ideal for trapping heat for the top of the head. A knit stocking or watch cap is also fine for this purpose, as are any number of insulated hunting caps. Something with ear flaps can be very essential in subzero weather. I gravitate to watch caps because even when pulled down over my ears I can hear what's going on around me. The insulated earflaps on most hunting caps restrict my hearing too much.

When it's really cold and there's a wind blowing, frostbite is just around the corner. To combat such conditions, especially on my face, I use a Balaclava (pullover face mask). The particular model I favor is the Fleece Face Mask made by Whitewater Outdoors, Inc. (W4228 Church St., Hingham, WI 53031, phone 1-(800) 666 2674). It has a face mask made of soft polar fleece and a hood of acrylic knit. One size does all. They come in various camo patterns or in solid white, which is handy for hunting in the snow. I bought mine from Cabela's for under $15. Cabela's also sells a variety of knitted watch caps.

I wear a knitted watch cap over the Fleece Face Mask to double the insulation on the top of my head in extra-cold conditions. Hair up there is thinner than it once was, so I'm taking no chances!

Most body heat is lost through head and hands. Covering the head, face, and neck will help ward off freezeout.

There's nothing worse than cold wind whistling down your neck. You can be covered from head to toe, but if your neck is bare you're in for a tough stint in a treestand. I beat the problem with a knitted acrylic Neck Gator, also designed to pull up over the mouth and nose if it gets really cold. I bought a new one last year for about six bucks from a local sporting goods store. The Neck Gator is another product from Whitewater Outdoors, Inc.

So now that you've prepared yourself for the Great White North, I have a little surprise for you. There's more to it than just being warm. You have to be quiet and you must not freeze to the tree in which you're sitting.

All the garments I've described thus far are amply warm and quiet. But there's still this matter of freezing to the tree. No, I'm not kidding. It really happens! As you sit in the extreme cold, clothed in breathing synthetic fiber clothing, the warmth of the moisture escaping from your clothing condenses when it hits the cold air. Then the condensation freezes. If you're sitting still for hours with your back against a tree, as happens in a treestand, you can be sure your upper body garment will freeze to the tree. Then, when your prize buck arrives on the scene and you attempt to shift quietly into a shooting position, you will have to tear the fabric away from the tree bark—and this will sound like the ripping of Velcro multiplied to the 10th power!

What's the answer?

A Tree Shirt!

Raven Wear to the rescue once more! They make a simple camouflaged polar fleece rectangle with straps to hold it to the tree. You simply attach the Tree Shirt to the tree where your coat will make contact and the Tree Shirt freezes to the tree instead of you. Neat, huh? An additional benefit is that it acts as a silencer between you and the tree

Odorless chemical hand and foot warmers are the greatest boon to cold weather hunters in years. They will generate heat for hours.

bark. I use mine in warm weather as well for that purpose. You can expect to pay about $30 U.S. for a Tree Shirt.

One last tip for you subzero treestand hunters. Before you head north, cut out a piece of scrap carpet to lay on the metal floor of your treestand platform. That thickness of carpet between the metal grate and your feet will do wonders. Contact with metal in subzero weather draws heat from your feet—or anything else—at an alarming rate.

Preparing Your Firearm

Now you're ready—if you've taken my advice so far. As a parting suggestion, I recommend you make sure all the oil or grease is removed from the inside of your rifle bolt before you go north. If you don't you'll likely become a frozen firing pin statistic. I recommend that you do not attempt to take a semiautomatic rifle into extreme cold.

McMillan offers a "Quiet Stock," made of fiberglass with a camou-flage flannel outer covering to mute the increased resonance of fiber-glass in extreme cold.

Once in camp, don't take the firearm indoors at all, or else condensation will form on the inner parts as well as on the scope lenses. If you take it inside, condensation will form. Then you'll take it outside and the condensation will freeze—and you're in for a heartache when you see your buck.

Another important tip to avoid last minute surprises is to put on all of the cold weather gear you plan to wear up north and then shoulder the rifle you intend to hunt with. You will probably discover both the eye relief and stock length have changed radically because of the bulk of your clothing. The scope will now be too far from your eye and your rifle's length of pull (distance from trigger to end of buttstock) will be too long. The average factory length of pull on rifles is about 13½ inches. This may have to be reduced by an inch or more to accommodate your "up north" clothing. I recommend purchasing spare stock you can cut down to the right length just for cold weather hunting. Synthetic stocks can be purchased to accommodate this need. The synthetics are especially great for cold weather hunting since they are impervious to the elements.

Having said that, there is one down side to most synthetic stocks in subzero weather. In bitter cold, synthetic stocks become extremely noisy to handle. You will be amazed at the amount of noise created by simply brushing your hand across a synthetic stock in extremely cold weather. The same motions may not make audible noise in warmer weather. In extreme cold, however, the stubble of your beard brushing against the stock as you shoulder your rifle for a shot will sound like coarse sandpaper grinding against hollow plastic. If your deer is close by, you're certain to get his attention! Such noises have often spooked deer before the hunter could get a shot.

The cure is simple: Buy a package of Dr. Scholl's Mole-Skin in the foot care section at your local drugstore and stick it to the stock where your face and hands will be making contact. The soft fuzzy surface of the flannel-like Mole-Skin will act as a perfect silencer on cold synthetic stocks.

The other option is to purchase a Quiet Stock from McMillan Fiberglass Stocks, Inc. (21421 N. 14th Ave., Phoenix, AZ 85027, phone (602) 582 9635). The Quiet Stock is a synthetic stock entirely covered with a camouflaged flannel fabric which silences noise effectively even in the coldest weather. Expect to pay about $295 for a custom drop-in fit, ready to screw into your barrelled action.

Rifle Slings and Other Horrible Things

Jeff sat in the tripod stand with his rifle resting upside down on the upper railing. When the buck appeared he

The Raven Wear Stand Bag is a highly insulated sitting bag that covers stationary hunters from feet to chest.

snatched the rifle from its perch, quickly turned it right-side-up and pulled it to his shoulder. Unfortunately, in the process of righting the rifle, the sling wrapped around the front of the scope and at the moment of truth Jeff couldn't see a thing. Another Canadian giant went unscathed because of the unexpected sling problem.

I think slings are fine for carrying rifles to and from deer stands, but as soon as I get settled in it comes *off*. Jeff's problem with the sling wrapped around his scope is just one of many sling problems I have witnessed. I know of several occasions where slings made squeaking noises at just the wrong moment when a buck was close enough to hear it. Each time, it spooked the buck before the hunter could get a shot. Remember, noises are accentuated and amplified in extreme cold weather conditions.

Although not a product of temperature, the most amazing sling tragedy I ever heard of occurred when a local fellow was driving down a farm road near his home in the country. He spotted a buck out in a field about 300 yards from the road, slammed on his brakes, shifted his floor-shift lever into neutral, grabbed his rifle from the rack behind the seat, and jumped out of the truck. Unfortunately his rifle sling looped over the gearshift lever and when he tried to pull the rifle out the door he inadvertantly shifted the still-running truck into low gear.

The truck lurched off down the road with the frantic hunter hanging on to his rifle and running for all he was worth alongside the truck. Before the race was over the truck ran off the road and through a fence, dragging its estranged driver into a windrow. No shots were fired and the buck is still at large. Of course, we should all understand that this wasn't so much the sling's fault as a graphic illustration of why deer hunting and vehicles don't mix! Truth is, though, that some of this "road warrior" hunting still goes on.

Cold Weather Deer Calling

A variety of effective deer calls are available these days and most of them are mouth-operated calls. You simply blow into them to get the desired sound, right? Wrong! Not in cold weather. Your warm breath flowing over a cold reed will result in a screeching sound more like a ruptured duck than a bleat or grunt. Mouth-operated calls must be used in reverse in cold weather. Instead of blowing the call, turn it around and *inhale* through it. This way you will be drawing cold air over the cold reed and no condensation will form. You will be able to call as often as you like with no ill effects. Just be sure you don't accidentally exhale your warm breath into the call. I inhale through the call, and then move it away from my mouth and exhale. It's as simple as that. Practice inhaling through your favorite call before you go north. You'll master it in no time and avoid a costly squawk at just the wrong moment.

Rattling Antlers in Cold Weather

Some southern hunters soak their rattling antlers in water or other secret concoctions before they go hunting. They believe they sound more realistic after a good soaking. Years ago I was guiding a nationally reknowned whitetail hunter in Alberta. He was from the southern U.S. and unbeknownst to me had soaked his antlers prior to his arrival. We crept up to the lip of a levee and gazed down on a dogwood willow thicket where I suspected a good buck was bedding. I nodded for him to begin rattling. He smacked his antlers together and they shattered like so much crystal. The water-soaked antlers had frozen and become as brittle as glass. The hunter looked at me and winced, as if to say, "It's too cold for human beings out here!" So, take a tip learned the hard way; don't soak your antlers in water if you plan to rattle up North!

There you have it . . . 25 years of research—mostly trial

and error—at your service! There's no reason to freeze out this deer season, no matter how cold it gets. Remember, dear reader, luck favors the prepared mind. So, as they say in the Boy Scouts, "Be Prepared!"

MANUFACTURERS AND SOURCES MENTIONED

Totem Outdoor Outfitters
7430-99 Street
Edmonton, Alberta
Canada T6E 3R9
(403) 432 1223

Icebreaker, Inc.
P.O. Box N
Clarksville, GA 30523
(706) 754 3732

Raven Wear of Canada
Box 411
Caroline, Alberta
Canada T0M 0M0
1 (800) 387 2836

Patagonia Mail Order, Inc.
P.O. Box 8900
Bozeman, MT 59715
(406) 587 7771

Bass Pro Shop
1935 S. Campbell
Springfield, MO 65898-0300
1 (800) 227 7776

Screaming Eagle, Inc.
P.O. Box 4507
Missoula, MT 2017
1 (800) 458 2017

Whitewater Outdoors, Inc.
W4228 Church St.
Hingham, WI 53031
1 (800) 666 2674

McMillan Fiberglass Stocks, Inc.
21421 N. 14th Ave.
Phoenix, AZ 85027
(602) 582 9635

La Crosse Footwear, Inc.
PO Box 1328
La Crosse, WI 54602

CHAPTER NINE

SUBTLE SECRETS
FOR MOVING DEER

Although many western Canadian guides are famous (if not infamous) for "pushing bush" (the Canadian term for deer drives), the noisy, obvious deer drives are seldom the most successful. The most consistent way to move a big whitetail buck into your crosshairs is to do it with such subtlety he never knows he's being moved. If he thinks he's making the decisions, you'll win—but if he thinks you're pressuring him to move, he'll beat you every time. Here are some time-proven tactics I employed in my outfitting days in western Canada that paid big dividends.

For me, deer hunting is almost like trapping. I like to hunt a specific buck which I know exists in a particular area, rather than just taking off blindly, in hopes of stumbling over just any deer. I want to study the animal, get a reading on what he does and where he does it, and, finally, I want to get him to step into an exact spot where I can see him, identify him, and have a clear shot at him. The same applies whether I hunt with a firearm or a bow. However, when bowhunting that "exact spot" becomes dramatically smaller due to the limited range.

Over the years I have played this cat-and-mouse game with many bucks. Often they came close, but not quite close enough to allow me a shot. So I engaged myself in the art of moving deer. This simply means I began to devise ways of making deer go where I wanted them to go without their knowing they were being influenced. That's tricky business, and it must be done with the utmost subtlety and finesse. As soon as a buck knows he's being pressured, he will turn against that pressure. It's a natural survival instinct, I'm sure.

The only way to successfully influence a buck to move in your desired course or direction is for him to choose that direction for himself. How many times have hunters tried to push a buck in this or that direction, only to have him turn against the pressure and do exactly the opposite of what the hunters wanted! That's the nature of the beast. But deer, like human beings, will take the path of least resistance if that path represents no danger. When I want to move a deer in a certain pattern or direction, I play upon this factor. I try to offer him an easier way than he already has. And I do it in such a way that the deer discovers it for himself, with no clues of my involvement.

While scouting for a particular buck along the edge of a large alfalfa field, bordered by heavy spruce and aspen timber, I noticed no less than a dozen well-worn game trails entering the east side of the field from the timber. Trying to anticipate which trail my buck would use was impossible. No one trail represented a more or less sensible choice than the other.

There was no livestock in the area, so I asked the farmer if he would allow me to wire two strands of barbed wire together to open a hole in his fence so the deer could pass through more easily. My idea was that this would create a single path of less resistance for the deer entering the field. With his blessing, I wired the two center strands of the four-strand fence to the strands above and below, opening a hole large enough for any deer to pass through with ease. I checked the "hole" two weeks later, and to my delight the

Thornberry believes that a traditional noisy deer drive like this is unlikely to produce results, especially if the quarry is a big buck. (Photo by Craig Boddington)

deer had funnelled virtually all of their travel activity right through it. The deer droppings and tracks in the snow made it obvious that it was now *the* trail.

I set up a stand in a large spruce tree beside that particular trail, and on the opening evening of the bow season, I arrowed the eight-pointer I was after. He came walking down the trail behind several does, without the faintest idea he was being duped. He was simply following the path of least resistance.

On another occasion I was trying to bowhunt a nice nine-point buck which I was certain would qualify for Pope and Young. The problem was that he and several other bucks were approaching the key alfalfa field through an open cow pasture where there wasn't a single tree large enough to set up a stand. To make matters worse, there wasn't any possibility of employing a ground blind, either.

Lesser bucks and does were using the trail past my big

Whitetail bucks seem to have an uncanny ability to sense when they're being pushed. If they think the movement is your idea, they're sure to resist and find another route. (Photo by Judd Cooney)

cottonwood tree every evening, but the larger bucks maintained their pattern through the open pasture, avoiding the trees like the plague.

It was interesting to note that I was hunting the prairie whitetail in the antelope country of southeastern Alberta.

The deer, like the antelope, were prairie creatures; it was obvious they felt safe when they were in the wide-open spaces. I was hunting the Red Deer River bottoms where the deer bedded in the impenetrable buffalo berry thickets. All the deer emerged from their bedding areas together, but as they started toward the alfalfa they hit a fork in the trail. Inevitably, the larger bucks took the fork that routed them through the open pasture, while the smaller bucks and does took the trail that passed through a sparse stand of ancient cottonwoods, including the one where I had my stand.

After a couple of days of watching this procedure, I was convinced that the buck I wanted wasn't going to use the trail through the trees. I watched the group of five bucks, including "my" buck, travel through the open pasture, jump the fence bordering the farm road, and then trot into the alfalfa field. They were using the same trail each day. Upon closer inspection, I found a deer trail worn deep into the earth where the bucks were crossing the fence. There were no other trails anywhere near this crossing. Now, how could I gently persuade the bucks to abandon this trail for the one that passed my tree—without them feeling that it was my idea?

The next evening a plan was born. I asked a friend of mine to accompany me for the evening. I parked my truck right against the fence where the bucks normally crossed. I asked my buddy to sit in the truck all evening. Then, when he saw the bucks emerge from the thicket, enroute to the crossing, he was to get out of the truck, slam the door, walk around the truck once, and get back in, slamming the door a second time. The idea was for him to be obvious to the bucks . . . and just as obviously in the middle of their crossing.

About four p.m. I headed for my treestand. When the

magic hour arrived all the deer emerged from the buffalo berry thicket as usual. Then, as was the custom, the bucks headed toward the open pasture while the others came my way. But, when my buddy started the door slamming routine, the herd of big bucks retreated into the thicket for a rethink of their program.

Since the response to the truck was left to their discretion, they didn't feel they were being trapped. They thought it over for a few minutes, and then they took the fatal trail past my tree. It cost the largest buck his life. He made P&Y with room to spare!

The plan worked because the buck got to choose the alternate trail. Had I tried to force them onto that trail, I'd still be waiting. It's important, when trying to move whitetails, to allow them to believe the choices they are making are all theirs. Otherwise it's a waste of time. They just won't play ball.

On another occasion I was bowhunting the northern edge of a mile-square alfalfa field. The deer bedded in the timber to the north of the edge I wanted to hunt. There were a dozen or more trails leading from the timber to the alfalfa, and the deer used them with no particular rhyme or reason. No matter which trail I overlooked, the bucks always used another. I knew they weren't spooked because they arrived in the alfalfa in broad daylight, regardless of which trail they chose. I had played my futile game of musical trails for a week, and not once did I pick the right one. I had one day of bowhunting left, and I had become obsessed with trying to pick the right trail. Bagging the buck, by this time, had become less important than just hitting the jackpot on my trail guessing game.

All the trails to and from the alfalfa field ran north and south, except one which looped in over a ridge from the northeast. It seemed that bucks would use this trail if they

When attempting to coax deer to use a specific route, the idea is to make it easier for them. Wiring a fence to create a gap (with permission from the farmer!) is a trick that has worked for the author. Deer will follow the path of least resistance right through the opening.

Raking a bare spot in the trail, then checking it, will quickly tell you which trail deer are using. Tilling the soil makes tracks easier to identify and date.

were in any way suspicious of a problem in the alfalfa field. The high approach enabled them to observe the entire field before entering it.

On the last day of bow season, since I had nothing to

lose, I decided to experiment with the deer. I purchased two bottles of Liquid Smoke. Normally used to give meat a smoked flavor while cooking, it's very potent-smelling stuff.

The wind was directly from the south. That meant it was blowing directly from the field into the deer's bedding area. I walked along the edge of the north edge of the field and upon every trail I poured the strong-smelling Liquid Smoke. All except the trail that came in from the northeast. That one I left alone, except for a treestand placed within shooting range.

All afternoon Liquid Smoke blew back into the bedding area, where I'm sure every deer bedded there must have thought the whole forest was on fire. Then, just before dark, deer began cautiously filtering in on the trail I was watching. My buck walked by me at 12 yards. I was proud of myself; I had outsmarted the whole herd!

I drew my arrow with confidence and cleanly missed my buck. Oh, well. At least I was watching the right trail! For that I could take full credit; I was able to alter their choice of trails without them realizing what was happening.

In bowhunting situations, where several trails followed a parallel course, I have occasionally blocked a given trail by falling a tree over it in a key place. This, if done well in advance (months, not days), will cause deer to use one of the other trails. In this manner I have reduced the odds on which trail the deer would take enough to move them past my treestand. Naturally such a move requires landowner permission for cutting down a tree. I prefer to cut a standing dead tree as opposed to a living tree if possible.

I have also been successful in pressuring deer to use alternate trails by hanging a white garment such as a T-shirt on a tree in plain sight of the trail I want the deer to abandon. The only problem with this is that the T-shirt represents something new and unnatural in their world. That worries deer. It might serve its purpose the first time the deer see it, but unfortunately it will likely cause some alarm and move them farther than intended. A fallen tree, on the other hand, is not uncommon to deer. The natural way is always the best in the long run.

Moving Deer with Bait

In wilderness settings, well away from livestock access, salt may have a magnetic effect on deer and other antlered game. In provinces where baiting deer is legal (British Columbia and Saskatchewan in particular), salt can be of great value in getting deer to work a specific travel pattern. This is especially true of areas where there is a sodium deficiency in the soil. To determine the sodium content, you can take a soil sample in for testing—but the far simpler way is to observe whether or not the nearest livestock to the area favor salt blocks. If they do, then deer will as well.

From a bowhunting standpoint, salt can be an exceptionally valuable means of establishing specific deer travel patterns. Salt attracts deer the best in the summer months when the weather is hot. At this time of the year the deer will lick salt frequently, sometimes several times per day. I have put salt blocks in the thick timber in the early summer or late spring, and by midsummer the deer are coming to it like candy. It's a simple matter of placing the salt block where you want the deer to come. Pick out a perfect tree for your treestand and place the salt 20 or so yards away.

In the early bow season, when the weather is still warm, the deer will continue to come to the salt regularly. As the fall weather cools, they respond less to salt. But as an early season attractant, it can be very effective. By placing the salt in thick timber, the deer feel covered and at home. Subsequently, they will visit the location much less cautiously than they would if it were out in the open.

If baiting is legal, salt is a perfect way to establish a travel pattern for the deer which you intend to bait later in the season, after the weather gets colder. If you have established a salt station during the summer months, the deer will be responding to that location all summer and into the early fall. Then, when the weather begins to cool, place your bait at the same location as the salt. The deer will already have established travel routes to the location, so as their interest in salt wanes, they will find the bait and continue with their travel pattern as already established.

Don't expect to put out bait for whitetails and have them find it overnight. Even if they do find it right away, they will be suspicious for a while—it's something new and different in their territory. Baiting with salt in the summer months gets the deer used to the location, and to the fact that there is something there that they want. Then when other bait is added, they will not be so suspicious. Remember, what you are trying to establish is a dependable travel route. It takes time to establish such routes. Last-minute efforts seldom produce the desired results. In fact, starting too late can work against you. Sudden changes in a deer's world often makes him avoid the disturbed area.

Monitoring deer activity around a bait station can be done in several ways. Naturally, you can perch yourself in a nearby tree and try to observe the deer visually. I don't favor this method because I don't want to be around the bait early or late in the day when the deer are most likely to be coming in (I'm talking about before the season opens). I'm a stickler for leaving the bait totally alone until I'm ready to hunt over it. So, I prefer to observe sign around the bait station in the middle of the day when the deer are in their bedding areas.

Tracks will tell you much about the size of the deer coming to the salt or bait station. Very large, splayed tracks will tell you a buck is frequenting the area. Occasionally I will take a garden rake with me when I go to a bait station. I will use the rake to loosen and turn the soil for a distance of about four feet on all incoming trails. This is especially helpful if the ground is dry and hard. Then, after a couple of days, I will observe the same trails. Deer tracks show up clearly in the soft, freshly-tilled earth.

As the rut approaches, bucks will rub trees and make scrapes all around the bait station. The bucks are keenly aware of the does concentrated in that area, so they make their sign accordingly. Rubs and scrapes will tell you plenty about the size of the bucks in the area, and you can figure all this out at midday without spooking the deer.

Baiting deer varies across the country. Some hunters use apples, some use carrots, some use other types of garden vegetables. My suggestion would be to use whatever type of bait the deer are accustomed to eating in any specific area.

In Texas, corn is the staple offering for baiting deer. The deer come to it like candy. I believe whitetails have an inherent craving for corn, even in areas where they have never seen or eaten it. Most of the Texas deer that come to bait corn have never seen it in other forms. They don't know where it comes from, nor do they care. They just know they like it, no questions asked.

In the western Canadian whitetail range I prefer barley to corn. The reason is that barley is a hot grain. By "hot," I mean high in protein. A little goes a long way, nutritionally speaking. Deer love it, but they can't eat a great deal of it at one feeding. Therefore barley lasts considerably longer

Hanging a piece of clothing saturated with human scent along a trail you don't want deer to use will deter them immediately.

than an equal amount of corn, which is not as hot. Another plus for barley is that deer will eat only a little of it as long as other browse is available. But after the first frosts fall, when the the tender broadleaf plants die, the barley becomes progressively more important to deer. When snow covers the ground, deer will be coming to barley regularly.

It is commonly believed that a big, mature buck is far too smart to come to a bait station. It's true, he's going to be more reluctant to do so than younger, immature bucks and does—but it does happen. I am aware of some huge bucks which have been taken over bait. If the bait represents danger to the buck, he's going to be shy. But if his feeding on the bait doesn't threaten him, he may be fairly vulnerable.

My strategy in baiting deer is always to attract and localize the does before the rut gets underway. If the does are regular patrons at the bait station, it's just a matter of time until a buck comes in to check the bait station for a hot doe. I have bagged several nice bucks on bait stations. The bait was not what brought them into range—rather, it was what kept the does where I wanted them. During the rut, if I can keep the does in sight I don't worry about where the bucks are. I know where they will be sooner or later.

Once I have deer coming to a salt station, I put out enough bait to last them two weeks at a time. Timing is important here. I'll be sure to put out plenty of bait two weeks before the first rutting behavior takes place, so that the does will be in position when the bucks get interested.

Baiting in the early fall is merely to let the deer know that the bait is there when they need it. Then, later in the fall, as the weather gets colder, they will simply come as a matter of routine. Routine is the key word for whitetails. As previously mentioned, many hunters try to bait in deer a day or two in advance. In most areas this is not enough notice for the deer to establish a travel route to the bait. The exception may be on some Texas ranches where deer run out onto the *senderos* every time they hear a vehicle go by, to see if it dropped any corn for them. This is the exception, not the rule.

This "deer highway" leads to a bait station where the deer have been feeding on barley. Baiting as practiced and legal in Saskatchewan is one of the most effective means of harvesting whitetails in the northern forests.

In any case, deer travel for three major reasons: for food, for cover, and to breed during the rut. In every case of influencing deer movement, the hunter will be dealing with one of these factors—possibly all three. The two keys to successful manipulation of deer movement are: (1) Always be subtle and, (2) Always let it be the deer's choice to move the way you want him to go. If it's his idea, he'll do it. If it appears to him to be your idea, chances are he'll resist it and go another direction.

The Circulation Drive

Deer drives, as a means of directing mature whitetail bucks to waiting hunters, offer about the same odds as winning a million at the roulette wheel in Vegas. The reason for the general lack of success in deer drives (I'm talking about mature trophies, not young bucks) is that the bucks feel the pressure of the drive by one means or another and understand that they are being pressured to move in a particular direction. Somehow they know it's not in their best interest to go with the flow.

A deer drive usually violates the second rule of manipulating deer movement . . . it doesn't allow the deer to choose according to his own desires. Suddenly he feels pressure and is bound to resist it. Very occasionally a big buck will find himself in a trap that offers him no other options, and a drive will work—but not often enough to bank on.

I've seen bucks beat deer drives in every imaginable way, including simply lying down flat against the ground and letting hunters walk right past them. Big whitetails are masters at this game. They have more answers for deer drives than most hunters have questions. However, quite by accident, I stumbled onto a type of drive that works ex-

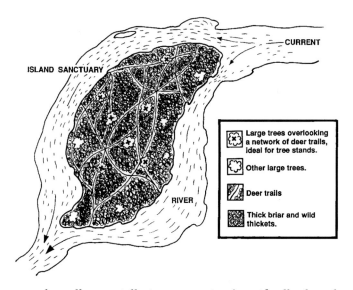

ISLAND SANCTUARY

CURRENT

RIVER

⊗	Large trees overlooking a network of deer trails, ideal for tree stands.
	Other large trees.
	Deer trails
	Thick briar and wild thickets.

tremely well, especially in sanctuaries (specifically densely timbered bedding areas) where a drive should never work. I call the system the "circulation drive." The following will explain how it was discovered and how it works.

Four hunters were placed in key ambush positions while it was still dark. Their guides showed them exactly where to hide and in what direction to be watching. Then the guides crept quietly away to regroup as pushers for the drive.

The drive was to take place on a 40-acre island lying in the Red Deer River channel in southeastern Alberta. The ice was a foot thick on the river, and there were an additional three inches of snow on top of the ice. The deer tracks in the snow left the tell-tale signs that several bucks were bedding on the island during daylight hours. According to their tracks, the bucks were leaving the refuge of the island thicket at night, as they prowled around in search of does. Then, as daylight approached, they would return to

The author arrowed this fine Saskatchewan buck during the rut. He was lured to a bait station by several does which were feeding there regularly.

the island where they were spending their days. The object was to get the bucks to step off the island in the light of day, so the hunters could see them.

We had been studying the island sanctuary for several days. It was a perfect bedding area, well out of the mainstream of the hunting pressure. There were a few old sprawling cottonwood trees on the island, but it was mainly covered with an interwoven tangle of rose briars, red willow, and snowberry bushes as high as a man's head. If not for the big, toe-dragging buck tracks crossing the river ice, we would never have suspected that there were any deer on the island.

With hunters positioned on points, my guides and I met at the narrow, eastern end of the island and waited for daybreak. There were five of us in all. Our plan was to spread out and move slowly down the island, making as little commotion as possible. We wanted to create subtle pressure to move the bucks.

We already knew from experience that if we were too obvious and generated too much pressure, the bucks would turn against us in the drive and beat us at our own game. Although we were seldom more than 20 yards apart as we made the drive, my guides and I seldom saw each other. The briar undergrowth was that thick. We could hear each other from time to time as the rose briars ripped at our clothing and tangled around our ankles, sometimes causing us to stumble.

We reached the midpoint of the island, but heard no shots. Systematically we proceeded, expecting to hear a deer break and run at any moment. The deer were moving. We knew that from the red-hot tracks everywhere. But when we broke out of the west end of the island, not one deer had left. We had made the best possible drive attempt to no avail.

We called our hunters out of hiding and they joined us as we walked back through the island to study the deer tracks. That was the most valuable part of the whole endeavor. It was amazing to find the beds where the bucks had been lying down—and then to observe how they had simply side-stepped us without ever being seen. It was truly incredible! At least five bucks had circulated around us without ever revealing themselves to a single man. They were "safer than a day in jail," as the saying goes, and they knew it. I'm convinced that a napalm attack wouldn't have moved those bucks off their island sanctuary.

When the season ended, we hadn't ruffled a single hair on any of the island bucks. That was a heartache. The huge rubs which abounded on the island indicated there were some old mossbacks camped there—but thus far they had us outsmarted.

During the course of the following winter I contemplated the island sanctuary . . . sometimes while awake, sometimes in my sleep. I knew there had to be some way to beat those bucks at their own game. But there was only one thing we could consistently cause those deer to do. We could circulate them around the island, but that was it. We could move 'em, but we couldn't get a look at 'em.

Sometime during the next spring the light came on; the idea surfaced. If we could circulate the bucks by making a slow drive, what would happen if we put our hunters in treestands throughout the island? They should be able to see what we, as drivers, couldn't. Wow! A plan was born.

The rifle season opened in early November, and by the middle of the month the ice was formed on the river again. The snow fell, and once again the tracks confirmed that the bucks were sticking with the same game plan as they had the previous year.

This time we had treestands in place high in the cottonwoods, offering our hunters a strategic view down into the thicket. We all knew we were on to something. This plan was going to be a whole new ballgame.

On the morning of the drive, we didn't bother getting to the island until well after daylight. We didn't have to hide so there was no need to get there in the dark.

At eight a.m. I sent the four hunters ahead to their stands. I allowed 30 minutes for them to get settled, and then we started the drive, exactly as we had done the year before. When it was over, to our utter disbelief, the results were the same as the year before. *Hunters, zero!* No one had seen a single deer. Repeating ourselves once more, we all walked back through the island and found fresh beds and tracks cirulating around the island. But not one fresh track came near a single cottonwood tree where hunters were sitting. It was an insulting defeat. These deer were starting to make me mad.

My guides and I pondered the disaster deep into the night, trying to find the missing piece of the puzzle. We had put the stands up during the late summer. All shooting lanes had been cut then so there was no fresh cutting to spook the bucks. The only thing we could come up with was the possibility that the bucks heard the hunters moving into position and were wise enough to avoid those areas—even as they were being moved around during the drive. Boy, that's giving deer a lot of credit! If our hunch was right, it serves as evidence that whitetail deer do have reasoning ability, regardless of what scientists say.

The next question was how to overcome this reasoning ability. Somehow we had to out-reason the deer. So far that was much easier said than done. It was getting to be a war of strategies. We were the ones who were supposed to have the superior mental capabilities, but thus far even that was hypothetical!

I spent a sleepless night studying the situation, and sometime during the wee hours of the morning, in a state of half-consciousness, it came to me. I bolted up in my bed and said aloud, "That's it! The hunters have to be part of the drive!"

Over breakfast I launched my brainstorm on the rest of the crew. I figured that if, the next time we approached the island, we let the hunters walk in with us as we made the drive, the deer wouldn't hear them coming in ahead of us. Assuming the deer couldn't count the number of drivers as the hunters passed their trees, they could climb quickly into their stands and just sort of disappear from the drive. The bucks would already be circulating as the drive got underway. There would be no broadcast of hunters climbing trees. The drive would start quietly and continue back and forth, from end to end of the island. Sooner or later it had to pay off.

For the first time I felt an excitement about the drive. I have tried to drive deer a thousand ways, and I have been snookered on most occasions. Does and small bucks were easy to drive, but big bucks play by different rules. They have an uncanny ability to find the one wrinkle in the plan—and hide in it. I wouldn't even have attempted to drive these island bucks except they were so static. They were always right under my nose. And of course, as their sign indicated, they were big, mature animals.

We waited several days before we tried the new concept. My strategy was that too much commotion too often might make the bucks abandon the island. Now, unlike my first attempt, I did not want the bucks to step off the island. I wanted them to stay within the confines of their sanctuary and circulate.

Thursday morning a total of nine hunters and guides assembled to try the new, improved "circulation drive." Each

The idea behind the "circulation drive" is to create natural movement and keep the deer circulating until they eventually drift past hunters strategically placed in stands. (Photo by Judd Cooney)

hunter knew which stand he was to occupy. They understood they would move onto the island abreast of the guides and move as quietly as possible toward their trees. Guides would keep moving after the hunters were aloft.

As we prepared for the drive I actually had butterflies in

my stomach. It reminded me of my high school football days, seconds before the opening kickoff. If this plan worked I would be a hero. If it failed, I would have had my nose rubbed in the dirt one more time. Win or lose, after this I was going to be fresh out of ideas.

Everybody lined up and started the shoulder-to-shoulder advance into the east end of the island. One by one, the hunters found their trees and climbed quietly into place, while the drive continued just as quietly without them.

My guides and I reached the west end of the island without hearing a shot. Somehow I expected it to work like that. I was not disappointed. When all guides were in view, I signalled them to do an about face and make another drive, this time from west to east.

During the initial drive, the bucks circled around us and headed into the drive as they had always done before. They sensed which way the drive was going and worked continually against it. Now they felt the eastward pressure and began circulating in a westerly direction.

Less than halfway into the drive a shot exploded from one of the cottonwoods. My heart leaped; the plan was working!

Hunters had been told to remain silent and aloft, even after shooting a buck. We were prepared to continue circulating the bucks for as long as it took to make the plan work.

Moments later, from farther east, a second shot rang out. That made two shots in less than a minute. I smiled and danced a silent jig. Now, a year and many sleepless nights later, our team was winning!

Our effort that day netted us two excellent bucks. But to me, more important than the two trophies was the fact of the matter: A well-organized circulation drive would produce!

That hunt changed forever my perspective on small, isolated sanctuaries. I mean the kind that are too thick to hunt from the ground, and too thick to drive deer out of.

Since that first success I have executed similar drives in many such sanctuaries with equally positive results. It takes advance planning with regard to treestand placement, and it takes the teamwork of a well-organized group of hunters and drivers. In this respect I had the distinct advantage of running a deer hunting operation which provided me with the required numbers of guides and hunters.

Even so, the bottom line is simply this: If you find a sanctuary where you know bucks are living, you can bet the bucks believe it's a foolproof (synonymous with hunter-proof) hideout. If there are trees big enough to hold tree-stands in or bordering the sanctuary, the deer have made one important miscalculation. Their sanctuary isn't really foolproof. A circulation drive will work . . . at least until whitetails learn to count!

ANTLER RATTLING TIPS FOR CANADA

Rattling antlers is not as productive per attempt in Canada as it is in the southern United States simply because there are not as many deer in Canada to hear the rattling. However, many Canadian areas have exceptional buck-to-doe ratios, which means that if the hunter handles the task right he has excellent prospects when a buck *does* hear the "horn rattlin'."

One of the major differences in successful rattling in Canada, as compared with the southern U.S., is that the deer are not apt to be drawn from their cover into the open where they can be seen. It seems that where deer numbers are fewer, the deer are all the more wary. Such is the case in Canada. For example, there are as many whitetails killed on the highways of Pennsylvania by automobiles each year as are killed by legal hunting in an average year in all Alberta. The annual whitetail harvest in Texas is 250,000 to 300,000 and that represents only about 10 percent of the Texas whitetail population. The annual Texas whitetail harvest exceeds the entire whitetail herd in Alberta! With this in mind, it's easy to understand why antler rattling is less successful per attempt in a Canadian province than might be the case on a large Texas ranch.

Now having said that, here's the good news. Though there are not as many ears to hear your rattling in Canada, when a buck does hear it, if you're doing everything right, I can't imagine a greater potential for success. In my 18 years of guiding and outfitting in Alberta I learned by trial and error which rattling techniques trick Canadian bucks and which ones don't. Follow these procedures next time you're in Canada and you may rattle in the bull of the woods.

The key to consistently successful antler rattling in Canada is to rattle from within the deer's sanctuary. The thicker the woods the greater protective cover it offers deer and the more secure they feel within its boundaries. It is from within the dense thickets that I rattle for Canadian bucks and it works!

Think about it for a moment. We tend to think that just because a buck heads for the timber at dawn and doesn't appear again until dusk that he's in the timber sound asleep in his bed all day. Nothing could be farther from the truth, especially during the rut. He'll be moving about within the safety of his sanctuary until light fades and makes him feel secure, or until the craze of the rut causes him to make a mistake. The fact is that once the homework is done and sufficient big buck sign has been located, it's time to rattle for him.

I won't belabor the issue of identifying big buck sign here, as there is plenty written on the subject already, but suffice it to say that where there's plenty of big buck sign, there's ample reason to expect the buck to be in that area again.

Once an area has been scouted to the hunter's satisfaction, and he is confident that there are good numbers of bucks there, he must then establish specific rattling locations within their territory. He must consider several factors when choosing his rattling sites.

One key factor is wind direction. Every area has at least

Although antler-rattling doesn't average as successful per attempt in Canada, the author believes this is because of low deer density. He believes rutty Canadian bucks will come to good antler rattling if they hear it. (Photo by Judd Cooney)

one dominant wind direction. The hunter should have several locations picked with wind direction in mind so that he can move into position without broadcasting his arrival. If rattling is done from the ground, that critical downwind view must be available. If, for example, the dominant wind direction in an area is from the northwest, the rattler will want a southeast view from his location in order to watch downwind. In almost all instances, an incoming buck will circle downwind of the rattling to prove with his nose what his ears are telling him. The hunter must be able to see the buck before it gets directly downwind and picks up his scent. Once the buck gets a whiff of the hunter, it's game over. So positioning is critical. That downwind view is essential. Should the wind blow from another direction, this site may be defeated. Thus the case for several rattling locations according to wind direction.

In the timber, the leaves covering the forest are noisy, like a carpet of corn flakes. Even the slippery whitetail cannot walk on dried leaves without making lots of noise. This gives me the added advantage of being able to hear an approaching deer . . . or an approaching hunter!

I follow well-worn game trails into the timber and watch for fresh rubs and scrapes as signs of buck activity. Once I find a circuit of scrapes, I begin looking for a logical position to rattle from. Bucks generally lay out a circuit of scrapes along some visual physical boundary within their territory. A fence line, creek bottom, or road allowance may be the physical boundary the buck uses to establish his scrape line.

The geographical boundary is seldom hidden. Once the hunter catches on to the kinds of boundaries the bucks use in laying out their scrape and rub lines, he will be able to spot likely territorial borders at a glance. Subsequently, he will be able to locate scrape circuits with ease. Such areas bucks use generation after generation if the landscape is not physically changed or altered. It is logical to expect to find scrapes in a given area year after year, even if a specific buck is killed. The landscape that appeals to one buck will likely appeal to others for generations to come.

I have found treasured spots where several bucks were making scrapes and rubs together. Within an area of 40 square yards there were over 20 scrapes of all sizes. The diamond willow bushes were literally shredded by rubbing bucks. A community scrape is far less common than individual scrapes, but once located, the hunter has all the cards stacked in his favor. He knows that numerous bucks frequent the area. The likelihood of two or more of the bucks arriving at the community scrape at the same time are very good. These areas will likely produce a nasty buck fight at some point during the rut. Rattling in such an area is very effective. The three-man team with the rattler on the ground and two hunters in treestands would be the perfect setup for such a spot.

I don't recommend rattling right over scrapes. I move away from them far enough so that I do not spoil them with human scent. I want the buck or bucks to continue to move freely along the circuit. For this reason I will look for the right spot 50 to 100 yards downwind of the scrapes and rattle from there. Bucks usually approach their scrapes from downwind, sometimes never coming nearer than 100 yards or so. A downwind position will be the most likely spot from which to intercept an incoming buck.

Once you have pin-pointed the exact spot from which you intend to rattle, you must make sure, if rattling from the ground, that you are in close proximity to the necessary small trees or bushes which you can rake with the antlers for realism. Also clear all twigs, branches, and leaves from the spot where you will be sitting or kneeling so that you can move without making any unexpected noise. Once all this is accomplished, your last consideration is blending in well with the habitat around you. I recommend dull earth-

The author rattling from his treestand, far up an Alberta aspen and deep within the whitetails' timber sanctuary.

tone clothing or camouflage, in wool or fleece fabrics if possible because they are the quietest. Be concealed well and absolutely quiet except when rattling.

Once I have settled into my ground position, I usually wait 15 to 30 minutes before rattling. I generally rattle from within a timbered area and I like to know that the forest has settled down after my arrival. No matter how quietly you approach your rattling position, squirrels, birds, and sometimes even deer become aware of your presence. When I sense that the other occupants of the forest have accepted or forgotten my presence, I am ready to begin.

The first step is the tickling of the tips of the tines. This is done by holding the antlers firmly in each hand and lightly clicking the tips of the antlers together. Tickling should last about 10 seconds. The function of this light, barely audible sound is to arouse the curiosity of any buck which may be lingering in close proximity to the rattler. If the rattling sequence begins with a mighty clashing of antlers, it may put the deer on the defensive and spook them away from the rattler, rather than attract them to him.

I learned this lesson well while rattling one evening from a treestand beside the Red Deer River in southern Alberta. I blasted the antlers together in a mighty clash and suddenly a half-dozen deer jumped into the river and swam quickly to the other side. Some hunters believe that the heavy rattling right off the bat is the way to attract a dominant buck, if he's in the area. By starting out with the light tickling of the tines, you will also get a look at what else is in the neighborhood. Not everyone has to kill the dominant buck to be happy.

After the initial tickling of the tines, wait a full 15 minutes before the next step. At this point, you are trying to kill a buck with curiosity. If there are no signs of life after 15 minutes, repeat the 10-second tickling sequence once again with slightly more volume. Again wait 15 minutes before continuing. The reason for such a short sequence followed by 15 minutes of silence is to maximize the deer's curiosity. Because the tickling sequence is lightly audible it is logical to assume that any buck hearing it will be relatively close to the rattler. For this reason I make the sequence short, to minimize the deer's ability to pinpoint the location of the sound.

I have actually watched a buck stand up in his bed upon hearing the first tickling of the antlers. As he tried to pinpoint the location of the sound, I stopped rattling. He stood like a marble statue without batting an eye, waiting for the next clue. Fifteen minutes later I began the next sequence. Immediately he began moving toward me. When I stopped again, he stopped as well. I waited in absolute silence for 25 minutes. Curiosity finally got the best of the buck and he came to within 30 feet of me, never knowing the real truth of the matter.

If there is a single common fault with most antler rattling, it is over-rattling. There are times when silence is golden. The time intervals between rattling sequences as described in this text are simply guidelines. I would not recommend that they be shortened, but when the situation calls for it, they may be lengthened as necessary. Every hunter who decides to take up antler rattling must learn that a whitetail buck is born with more patience than a human will ever achieve. Rattle accordingly. Make the silence work for you.

Now I want to make a most important point. Immediately after you finish a rattling sequence, put the antlers down and pick up your rifle or bow. This eliminates the horrible embarrassment and frustration of watching your buck appear while your hands are full of antlers. I rattled in my first buck at the tender age of 13. He charged in unexpectedly. With bloodshot eyes and hackles bristling, he stood 50 feet before me. I sat helplessly with antlers in hand and fear pounding in my heart. 'Nuff said!

If neither of the initial tickling sequences have produced any interest, approximately 30 minutes should have elapsed, and you are ready to begin rattling in earnest. When two mature, evenly-matched bucks square off for battle, it is serious business—sometimes to the death. This kind of fighting is not to be confused with the sparring lesser sub-dominant bucks which may appear more as play than battle. When two large, evenly-matched bucks commit to battle, it begins with a head-to-head charge and the subsequent striking of antler against antler, which I call the "clash."

I imitate the clash with a hard crack of the antlers. Once the bucks are engaged, antler to antler, they lunge to and fro and twist their heads in an attempt to throw the opponent off his feet. The initial clash is followed by the sound of antlers twisting and grinding, which is accomplished by twisting the wrists and grinding the antlers against one another. This sequence should produce an erratic, non-rhythmic variation of sounds. Two bucks engaged in battle may stand head to head and push silently for a moment, then one buck will shake his head furiously, intensifying the clattering of antlers. Picture the fight in your mind as you recreate it with antlers.

While the antlers are producing the all-important sound of the fighting bucks, the rattler (if he's on the ground) should be kicking leaves and working his antlers against bushes or tree bark at the same time. The fighting is furious in reality and there are eight feet in constant motion, driving, skidding, and thrashing the ground. The rattler wants to recreate the whole scene as if he is going to do it

The author and longtime friend Phillip Harrison with a buck rattled in for Harrison at dawn along the willow-choked banks of the Battle River in eastern Alberta.

justice. Once the battle is underway, there is no such thing as too much noise.

After approximately 30 seconds of this twisting and grinding of antlers and thrashing the leaves and nearby shrubs, separate the antlers with a loud clatter of tines as the antlers are jerked apart. Imagine the bucks pulling away from each other with a violent shaking of their heads. Picture that move in your mind's eye and imitate it when you break the antlers apart.

Immediately following the break, rake one antler vigorously against a tree trunk for 10 seconds. Bark raking is a common occurrence among fighting bucks. I have watched them suddenly turn from one another and vent their wrath upon a tree trunk or sapling. I'm not sure of the significance of bark raking, but it is not the same as rubbing. It appears to be an act of rage among fighting whitetails so I incorporate it into my rattling sequence.

Immediately after the 10-second bark raking sequence, holding the bases of the antlers firmly in both hands, strike the butts of the main beams against the ground in a two-part rapid sequence, recreating the "forefoot alarm/challenge." This rapid thump-thump striking of the forefoot against the ground is used as a challenge or alarm signal. Both bucks and does use this signal so I imitate it as part of rattling repertoire. The following five steps will summarize my entire rattling sequence from a ground position:

1. *Tickling Tines.* Holding the antlers firmly, tickle the tips of the tines together as a teaser to arouse the curiosity of a nearby buck. Tickling should only last 10 seconds. Wait quietly for 15 minutes and then repeat the tickling sequence with slightly more volume for another 10-second period. Wait an additional 15 minutes. If no success, move ahead to step two.

2. *The Clash.* An initial crack of the antlers imitating the initial charging together of two bucks.

3. *Twisting and Grinding.* Immediately following the clash, twist and grind antler against antler for approximately 30 seconds. Accompany the twisting and grinding with the thrashing of leaves and breaking of branches to imitate the sound made by the deer's feet during combat. End this sequence with an obvious break.

4. *Bark Raking.* Immediately following the 30-second twisting and grinding sequence, rake one antler vigorously against a nearby tree trunk or sapling for 10 seconds.

5. *Forefoot Alarm/Challenge.* Upon completion of the bark raking sequence, the forefoot alarm/challenge is simulated by a rapid two-part pounding of the butts of the antlers against the ground, creating a "thump-thump" sound.

Steps two through five should take approximately 50 seconds. After completion, quickly put the antlers down and pick up your bow or rifle. Wait at least 15 minutes before repeating steps two through five again. If you have any indication of an approaching buck it is wise to remain absolutely silent rather than continuing to rattle. A whitetail buck will attempt to pinpoint your location through his sight, smell, and hearing. The less understanding he has of your exact location, the less likely you will be caught flat-footed.

The question of how long to continue rattling in one spot arises after an hour or so with no success. If you were in Texas, you'd try a rattling site for just a half-hour or so, then head for the next spot. However, in Canada, if you have done your homework and have reason to believe there is a buck inhabiting the area, you cannot rattle too long from one spot. Deer move in and out of the audible range of the antlers. Once, after rattling for four hours in the same spot, a 10-point buck came in on the dead run, nearly stepping on my brother, John. It was obvious that the deer had simply wandered into hearing range of the antlers, and upon picking up the sound, he came in a mad dash. It is important to realize that you will not be aware of every buck which responds to the antlers. Quite often they will figure the rattler out and slip away totally unnoticed. If you lose faith in your position you should move at least a half-mile to a new spot before beginning again.

Rattling from a treestand has some obvious limitations when compared with rattling from the ground in that much of the sounds of battle cannot be recreated. The thrashing of leaves and branches and the forefoot alarm/challenge are examples of sounds which will be eliminated when rattling from above. Nonetheless, treestand rattling can be extremely effective. The rattling sequence begins the same in the treestand as it does on the ground. The 10 seconds of tickling the tines followed by

Raking tree bark with an antler produces the sound of a buck rubbing a tree. This sound will often cause a buck to come over for a look.

15 minutes of silence begins the sequence. Repeat this if there is no response the first time. If, after 30 minutes and

Pounding the ground twice in rapid succession with the butts of the rattling antlers imitates the alarm stomp or challenge and helps round out the variety of sounds made by real fighting bucks.

two tickling sequences, there are no results, you are ready to begin the heavier rattling sequence.

Begin with the clash, as previously described, followed by the twisting and grinding sequence for approximately 30 seconds, ending with the break. Now put down your antlers and pick up your bow or rifle. You will need a logical place to put the antlers when not in use; it's not quite as simple as when rattling from the ground. Hanging antlers over a limb can be tricky. They have a tendency to swing and clack together in the wind, which can ruin all your efforts. Plan ahead and know where the antlers are going to be placed. You will want to be able to pick them up and discard them quickly and quietly.

When you have completed the treestand rattling sequence, which includes the clash, twisting and grinding, and break, you will have consumed approximately 35 seconds. Wait 15 minutes and repeat the same sequence. Hereafter, I recommend the rattling sequence be repeated at 30 to 45-minute intervals. Again, if you have done your homework and believe in your location to begin with, don't give up and leave after an hour or so.

I have rattled from one stand for four or five hours before a buck responded. The buck wasn't ignoring me the whole time; he just finally happened into earshot and took the bait. If the area was good enough to pick for rattling in the first place, it will be no less valuable a few hours later. Stay with it and eventually you will hit the jackpot. What applies in Texas may not apply to successful rattling in Canada, but this adaptation of rattling will work anywhere in North America where the buck-to-doe ratio is close.

CHAPTER ELEVEN

CANADIAN WHITETAIL RIFLES: MASTERING THE LONG SHOTS

Since deer hunting habitat in Canada ranges from dense timber to open prairie, no one rifle is ideal for all situations. It's essential to deal with both extremes, so in this chapter we'll deal with the long-range rifle; our final chapter will address choosing the ideal thicket or brush rifle for close shooting in tight timber.

The huge buck suddenly popped into the endless stubble field from a blind draw. "How far out there is he?" whispered the desperate hunter.

"Just shy of 400 yards," answered the equally anxious guide.

"Where should I hold?" the hunter questioned.

"Where is your rifle zeroed?" asked the guide. Meanwhile the opportunity evaporated into thin air as the great deer vanished into the timber. This sad scenario is not uncommon, and many fine trophies are still at large because these questions were left unanswered until it was too late. Here's how to answer them before they cost you the trophy of a lifetime.

As the focus of whitetail hunting broadens from east to west and south to north, the terrain changes radically. Up-

Much of western Canada's whitetail range is wide-open country and shots can be long—especially at big bucks. (Photo by Craig Boddington)

state New York hunters may be overwhelmed by the wide open spaces of Alberta.

That little .308 semiauto that was so handy in the dense thickets of the East may suddenly be less than ideal when a real buster comes rolling across the western prairie at an unknown range. The fact is that whitetails at long ranges (250 to 400 yards) are a common fact in the western Canadian provinces. It is also interesting to note how often the largest buck is seen at the longest distance. I spent 18 years guiding whitetail hunters where wide open spaces are common. In an effort to prepare my hunters for the kinds of shooting conditions they might encounter, I had to develop a system of range calculation that was quick, reliable, and easy to grasp.

I was preparing for an antelope hunt many years ago, and I knew that shots might be longer than I was used to making. I made a life-sized, plywood antelope silhouette and propped it up at a measured 400 yards for shooting

Accuracy is the first requirement for a long-range rifle. Optimally the rifle should be capable of one minute of angle (MOA), meaning one-inch groups at 100 yards. (Photo by Craig Boddington)

practice. I had a 2-7X variable scope with Duplex cross hairs on my 7mm Remington Magnum. With the scope cranked up to 7X, I looked at the antelope silhouette and was delighted to find that the heavy inner ends of my horizontal Duplex crosshairs framed the silhouette perfectly fore and aft.

In other words, one heavy crosshair ended right at the antelope's rump and the opposite crosshair ended flush with the front of his chest. Immediately I realized I had stumbled onto a great way to pinpoint distance by using my crosshairs as a rangefinder.

I moved to 300 yards and twisted the adjustment ring on my scope until I framed the silhouette again. It was obvious that with a little homework I could pre-establish the necessary power settings to determine any range I wanted to find—as long as I could see a broadside view of the game I was hunting.

A bipod is an invaluable tool for long-range shooting, especially in the prairie country where natural rests may be scarce. (Photo by Russell Thornberry)

Longer barrels are coming back into vogue, and they're ideal for open country whitetail hunting. This is Remington's "Sendero Special" Model 700, available in several hard-hitting calibers. (Photo courtesy Remington Arms)

Since that day I have effectively used my variable scopes (always with Duplex reticles) to calculate distance in all types of hunting. I have a beautiful Dall sheep on my wall which I dropped with a single shot at 400 yards, across a deep canyon in the Northwest Territories with nothing but eagle pasture between me and the sheep. I had done my homework with a sheep silhouette before the hunt, and when I cranked up to 7X and took a look, the guesswork was over. Had I not done my homework, I would have had no idea how far away that sheep was.

My rangefinding system has benefitted numerous of my whitetail hunters in Alberta, where long shots can be the name of the game. Most hunters, when initially exposed to

LONG RANGE CALIBER SELECTION CHART

CALIBER	BULLET WEIGHT (GRAINS)	BULLET DESIGN	MUZZLE VELOCITY (FPS)	ENERGY @400 YARDS (FT-LBS)	TRAJECTORY CURVE (300 YARD ZERO) MAX HT.	DROP AT 400 YDS
.25	120	SPITZER	3200	1522	4.1"	10.0"
6.5mm	120	SPITZER	3200	1417	4.1"	10.0"
6.5mm	140	SPITZER	3000	1577	4.4"	10.0"
.277	130	SPITZER	3200	1488	4.2"	10.2"
.277	150	SPITZER	3200	1930	4.2"	10.1"
7.0mm	140	SPITZER	3200	1698	4.2"	10.0"
7.0mm	154	SPITZER	3200	1935	4.0"	9.7"
.308	150	SPITZER	3200	1605	4.3"	10.3"
.308	165	SPITZER	3100	1813	4.4"	10.4"

this range-finding concept, are simply shocked to find that they can plunk their bullets consistently into a six or eight-inch circle (and often much less!) at 400 yards! As long as the hunter uses an accurate rifle capable of delivering the bullet speed and energy necessary to make a clean kill, it's a simple system to learn and utilize—and it will enable you to make shots at ranges you may have thought impossible.

The key to long-range shooting begins with a rifle capable of minute-of-angle accuracy, basically one-inch groups at 100 yards. The next requirement is bullet speed. A rifle bullet literally runs a race with time as gravity pulls it toward the earth. The faster the bullet, the farther it will travel before gravity finally overcomes it.

Determining a proper criteria for bullet weight and speed for long-range shooting is fairly simple. We want to be able to aim at the deer, not over him or under him, and make every shot fatal from zero to 400 yards. To accomplish this we will most certainly have to zero our rifles at 300 yards.

For the calibers I have recommended on the "Long Range Caliber Selection Chart," this means rifles will be sighted in from 3 to 3½ inches high at 100 yards, depending on the particular cartridge. In addition, our cartridge must deliver its bullet to the 400-yard mark without rising more than five inches above or 12 inches below our line of sight. Remember, we want to be able to aim directly at the deer at all distances out to 400 yards. Many times I have watched panic-stricken hunters miss deer because they felt they had to hold high or low. In jest I have offered them this suggestion: "Aim at the deer first. If that doesn't work aim at something else!"

For whitetail deer, even the large Canadian whitetails, 1500 foot-pounds of energy is more than adequate for a clean kill, given proper bullet placement. For this purpose

A new version of the old Savage Model 110 is their Model 112 FVSS "Long Range Rifle," in stainless featuring a 26-inch fluted barrel and synthetic stock. (Photo courtesy Savage Arms)

Left to right, 7mm Remington Magnum, .270 Winchester, .280 Remington, .30-06, .300 Winchester Magnum. Within reasonable limits the exact cartridge chosen for long-range work isn't as important as the rifle's accuracy and the hunter's ability with it. (Photo by Craig Boddington)

I recommend the calibers shown on my chart, as well as a specific range of bullet weights for each, plus minimum muzzle velocities. Note that my chart is for *calibers*, not specific cartridges within a caliber. There may be several cartridges in a given caliber that will make the grade, such as the .25-06 Remington and .257 Weatherby Magnum within the .25 calibers, and so forth. Note, also, that spitzer (sharp-pointed) bullets must be used. Given aero-dynamic bullets, any of the recommended caliber/bullet weight combinations travelling at the stated muzzle veloci-ties will arrive at 400 yards with more than enough punch for even the largest whitetails.

You will notice on the chart that calibers less than .25 have not been included. The limitation is their very light bullet weights, which are incapable of delivering the neces-sary foot-pounds of energy at long range.

A quick study of the Long Range Caliber Selection Chart makes an obvious case for magnum power and velocity for long-range shooting. It is also interesting to note the addi-tional foot-pounds of energy delivered at 400 yards by the 150-grain .270 bullet as well as the 154-grain 7mm bullet. This is due to the superior ballistic coefficient (a measure of a bullet's ability to overcome air resistance) of these par-ticular bullets.

I have expressed the ideal calibers in terms of bullet di-ameters, weights, and velocities rather than cartridges, and there's little reason to specify particular makes and models of rifles. Accuracy as well as velocity vary greatly among in-dividual rifles, even between identical rifles with identical loads. Naturally, makes and models of rifles are not the issue here, but rather how they perform. The ballistics re-flected in the chart can be achieved in popular magnum ri-fles offered by the majority of American gunmakers.

Once the hunter has selected the right rifle and cartridge for the job at hand, his next concern should be the right scope. The scope design is all-important because it will ac-tually be used as a range-finding tool. Any variable scope ranging from 2X or 3X up through 10X will work well, providing it comes with "plex-type" reticles. Almost every scope company has its own trade name for this reticle, but we're speaking of a reticle with coarse outer crosshairs on the perimeter and very fine crosshairs in the center. This does not mean tapered crosshairs. It is important that the heavy crosshairs stop abruptly where the fine crosshairs begin. For rangefinding purposes I recommend scopes of no less than 7X at the high end. Variable scopes with a top end of 9X or 10X will work just as well.

It should be mentioned here that precision long-range shooting is virtually impossible without a light, crisp trigger pull. Most factory rifles come off the shelf with triggers set from five to as much as eight pounds. That is simply too much trigger for precision long-range shooting. Most factory triggers are adjustable, at least on bolt-action rifles. Some can be adjusted down to a clean, travel-free three-pound pull, but some cannot. If the trigger on your rifle cannot be set crisp and safe at three pounds, then you should consider one of the excellent adjustable custom aftermarket triggers. On my own rifles I have used both Canjar and Timney triggers and have been very pleased with both.

To shoot my best, especially at long ranges, my trigger must be an afterthought; never something I have to concentrate on. I must never be aware of trigger travel or pressure. When my shot is ready, the trigger must move automatically and effortlessly, as if it were part of my body. If the trigger becomes the object of my concentration, my aim will suffer. Talk with competitive benchrest shooters and all will tell you that trigger pull is one of the most critical aspects of their shooting.

A word of caution about adjusting triggers. If they are set too light, a sudden jar could cause them to fire. And for that reason I always have a qualified gunsmith adjust my triggers. I recommend that you do the same rather than risk an unsafe condition.

Next the hunter must make the all-important silhouette target. Heavy cardboard or 1.4-inch plywood will be the ideal material. Be sure that you get the dimensions right for the deer you intend to hunt. Obviously an 80-pound Texas Hill Country deer silhouette isn't going to prepare you for shots at big 300-pound northern deer. I have measured countless Alberta bucks from stem to stern and I find they average about 48 inches in body length, when standing or walking.

The slickest way to make your silhouette is to get a clear 35mm slide of a buck standing broadside to the viewer and project it onto your target material and trace it to the desired dimensions. One slide can be enlarged to whatever size you need, and it gives a perfect silhouette.

The initial target practice from zero to 400 yards should be done from solid benchrest positions to establish precise points of impact at various ranges. Many rifle ranges do not offer all the space needed for this exercise, but it doesn't take much to build an adequate portable bench that can be taken out to the farm for practicing. Once the shooter knows, in absolute terms, where his rifle will shoot at all ranges, as well as what specific scope settings identify those specific ranges, he should abandon the benchrest and practice shooting from more typical field positions. I personally like to use a detachable bipod rest from either prone or sitting positions. The bipod gives me a rock-solid rest just about anywhere.

Learning to get into a solid, rested shooting position as quickly as possible is as important as the shooting itself.

As you practice looking at your silhouette through your scope at various ranges, the computer of your mind is programming that distance to memory. You learn to know at a glance how to judge the distance to your target—even before you make the final calculation through the crosshair

400 yds.

The heavy ends of the horizontal Duplex crosshair frame the buck fore and aft at 400 yards, in this case with the 2-7X scope turned up to 7X. By learning at what distance the deer is framed at a certain power level you have a very fast and sure rangefinder.

adjustment. This is why ongoing practice is so beneficial. We learn from continual experience.

Another handy tip is to write down the proper scope settings that identify specific ranges. Tape this information to

300 yds

A

At 300 yards with the scope still on 7X the target flows over the ends of the Duplex crosshairs. In a hunting situation the shooter would know instantly that his buck is less than 400 yards.

your gunstock in a place where you can refer to it quickly in case you get rattled and forget it. This can happen under the pressure of seeing a monster-class buck.

Using the ballistic performances described in the chart, shooters will find that they can hold at the center of the deer's ribs out to 300 yards and make a killing shot. At 400 yards, hold high on the shoulder, just below the hairline of the deer's back, and you will achieve a center rib shot. There is only one adjustment in point of aim required between zero and 400 yards, and that is at or near 400 yards.

For this reason, with my particular scope, when I want to determine the range of a distant whitetail, I turn my variable adjustment to 7X before I even look at the deer. I know that by observing my target at 7X I will instantly be able to establish whether the deer is more or less than 400 yards. That is my most important calculation. If he is less than 400 yards away, I will hold on the center of his ribs. If he is a full 400 yards away, I will hold at the top of his shoulder. If he is more than 400 yards, I will pass on the shot. My initial observation at 7X will give me all that information instantly. Naturally, the specific 400-yard setting may vary from one make of scope to another, and each hunter must establish the proper magnification setting for himself.

The beauty of this system is that one look through the scope tells you what you need to know. And as quickly as you establish the critical range information, you are ready to shoot. There are no knobs to turn, or extra time-consuming instruments to fiddle with. You simply read the range, aim, and shoot—all in one fell swoop.

I have established 400 yards as a maximum range because of the dramatic bullet drop beyond that distance. I feel that all hunters have a responsibility to take shots within the parameters of their absolute abilities. In my opinion, shots beyond 400 yards stretch the capabilities of both men and equipment.

Long-range shooting is a rifleman's game and there is no substitute for a super-accurate rifle and lots of practice. In truth, most hunters are unsure of distance at ranges in

450 yds.

C

At 450 yards there is visible daylight between the ends of the Duplex crosshairs and the target. By experimenting with the variable adjustment ring, you may also determine which magnification settings frame a buck at 200 and 300 yards. Write down the data and tape it to your gunstock until you have it memorized.

excess of 150 yards. A trip to the rifle range generally offers a 100-yard target which, because of experience, becomes the hunter's only frame of reference for distance. But with practice that can be changed quickly. I have tutored many hunters in the art of long-range shooting. Given an accurate rifle, I have never yet had a failure. Give this system a try before you head for the Canadian prairies for your dream hunt and stack the odds in your favor—even at ranges you may have once thought beyond your reach.

Oh yes, in closing may I suggest you take a good, dependable bolt action rifle when you go. I have heard all the arguments in favor of the semiautos, and I have watched those same rifles freeze up in severe cold and cost their bewildered owners the trophy of their lives. Trust me: In extreme cold bolt actions are the name of the game!

CHAPTER TWELVE

CANADIAN WHITETAIL RIFLES: THICKET RIFLES

That long-range powerhouse may be a match made in heaven for the open prairies, but in thick timber with limited visibility, a close-range precision sniping tool is just what the doctor ordered.

A thicket gun, you ask? Is that another way of saying brush gun? No, not in the traditional sense. The term "brush gun" has always been applied to some form of short-barrelled carbine firing bullets as heavy as golf balls in the hope of bulldozing through twigs, limbs, and small trees. The truth of the matter is that the traditional brush guns such as the .30-30, .35 Remington, and .45-70 have always been a bit mythical in terms of what they would or would not do in heavy brush. There have been some extensive tests run on the slow-moving, heavy bullets in heavy brush, and each test indicates that such cartridges do not perform as well as the zippier, flat-shooting cartridges such as .243 and .270 Winchester.

I must point out that while the faster calibers managed to hit closer to their intended point of impact when fired through a maze of multi-sized hardwood dowels than did the slower "brush" calibers, *nothing* could be considered dependable when fired through obstructions. It might be said that the brush gun concept is not only a myth, but an irresponsible concept at best. Back when "brush guns" were first hitting the market, in the 1800's, the only calibers in existence were the slow, heavy types. It's not that the old-timers were irresponsible in their choice of calibers. It's just that they had no other choices. Slow, heavy bullets were all that was available for a long time.

A short-barrelled carbine with a fast action makes sense in thick timber, in terms of a rifle that can be managed in tight places. But the idea of a bullet bulldozing its way to a target with any dependable degree of accuracy is simply hopeful thinking. A responsible hunter will not gamble on his shot. He wants a clean kill or nothing.

"How can I argue with the untold thousands of deer killed in the brush with traditional 'brush guns'?" you may ask. I don't argue at all. I simply say that the vast majority were taken with clean shots that had no deflection. It's easy to claim success when the deer is on the ground! But if we could measure the number of bullets deflected in the brush throughout modern deer hunting history, bullets that never touched their intended target, the success of the brush gun might not appear so certain.

Although what I call a "thicket gun" may be used for the same type of hunting as the traditional "brush gun," the criteria is not the same. A thicket gun, according to my personal criteria, is certainly going to be used in the thickest kinds of timber and underbrush—but is not intended to be a bulldozer. Rather, it must be a fast-handling, deadly accurate, close-range sniping rifle—with plenty of knockdown power. Instead of trying to plow a bullet through a tangle of limbs and branches, I want to be able to pick out even the most minute hole and shoot through it without even tickling the smallest twig.

A thicket gun, used as it is intended, should be a one-shot rifle. That is not to say that the rifle should not be capable of more than one shot, but one shot should be all

The truth is no bullet is particularly reliable if you attempt shots through brushy obstructions—not even the famed "brush calibers." Far better to wait until the buck is clear, or try to find even a tiny hole to shoot through. (Photo by Judd Cooney)

that is needed to do the job right. For this reason, and because of the need for pinpoint accuracy, I personally prefer a bolt action or perhaps one of the excellent modern single shot carbines.

Accuracy is generally described in terms of how well a rifle groups several shots at 100 yards or more. However, with a thicket rifle, I suggest being zeroed at 50 yards. Many rifles capable of very tight groups at 50 yards might be less accurate at longer ranges. My own criteria is simple; I want a rifle that will shoot each shot into the same hole at 50 yards. I stick with bolt actions and single shots, which offer superior accuracy at all ranges. However, it all boils down to the accuracy of an individual rifle. Some lever actions produce perfectly acceptable accuracy at the limited ranges required of a true thicket gun.

Another consideration that relates to actions is gun weight. Almost all of my thicket hunting is done from treestands. I prefer a rifle that is short, light, and easy to handle. A 20-inch barrel is plenty long enough for my purposes. Short-action cartridges such as the .308, .284, and 7mm-08 offer plenty of punch and allow the use of shorter, lighter bolt actions. The short action eliminates some weight and reduces the overall length of the rifle, making it more compact. This is a desirable and essential virtue in a thicket rifle. I consider 40 inches a maximum overall length for the ideal thicket rifle, and I prefer a total weight of seven pounds or less, including the weight of the scope.

Since hair-splitting accuracy is essential to facilitate tricky shots in dense brush, a scope is absolutely mandatory. But low-power scopes are the order of the day. Low magnification allows plenty of light transmission in dense brush where light is often low to begin with. In addition, low-power scopes allow full vision of small objects such as twigs or blades of grass, even at close range. The higher the power of magnification, the more such potential obstructions are dissolved from view. The ideal scope for a thicket gun should offer from 1X to 1½X on the low end to a maximum of 5X magnification on the high end. A fixed 1½X is also an excellent choice. A little magnification is far better than too much; I find top quality variables in 1–5X range ideal for thicket hunting. Such scopes are typically smaller and lighter than their more powerful cousins, contributing to lighter overall gun weight.

Choice of reticle is important. The hunter must maximize his ability to see, so I prefer a fine crosshair as opposed to a plex-type or post reticle. I want to see as much as possible through my scope, so the less space occupied

Marlin's lever action 444S in .444 Marlin is a classic brush gun and a good one. Its big cartridges anchor deer well, but it's no better than a lighter caliber for getting through brush. (Photo courtesy Marlin)

by the reticle, the better. All shots are going to be at relatively close range so seeing the crosshairs clearly will not be a problem.

As a final note on scopes for a thicket rifle, I suggest that the lowest possible scope mounts be used. You want the line of sight and the path of the bullet to be as close together as possible. The less distance between the line of sight and the path of the bullet, the less likelihood of unexpected bullet deflection from twigs or branches that appeared to be out of the line of fire.

With the influx of plastic and fiberglass stocks, even the heftier rifles can be reduced in weight. In addition, synthetics offer more consistent accuracy in that they are impervious to all weather conditions. A synthetic stock may knock as much as a full pound off the overall weight of your favorite rifle, as well as tighten up accuracy. Drop-in, synthetic stocks are readily available for most current factory rifles, and most manufacturers now offer synthetic-stocked models over the counter.

Accuracy is the all-important key in a thicket rifle—as it should be in any hunting rifle. However, fine-tuning accuracy can mean more than just the barrel, stock, or choice of ammunition. I find that one of the most critical and yet often overlooked ingredients to accuracy is the trigger. This is just as important in thicket rifles as it is for long-range

Short, light bolt actions like this Remington Model Seven FS (Fiberglass Stock) are the author's choice for thicket hunting. Mated to a .308 Winchester firing 180-grain bullets, he finds such a rig handy, accurate, and powerful enough for any whitetail. (Photo courtesy Remington Arms)

rigs. Again, I adjust my triggers to a three-pound pull—and if my gunsmith can't adjust the trigger to a safe, reliable three-pound pull, I have the factory trigger replaced with an aftermarket trigger like a Timney or a Canjar.

No writing on deer rifles would be complete without due attention to calibers, and I certainly have my pets where the thicket rifle is concerned. I am fond of short-action cartridges such as the .308, .284, and the 7mm-08. However, my selection of these cartridges reaches beyond action length. I also believe in moderate speed as opposed to magnum velocity when it comes to thicket rifles. By this I mean that I prefer bullet velocities between 2500 and 2800 feet per second at the muzzle, and just about the same speeds at point of impact. In addition, I am convinced that bullet weights ranging from 150 to 200 grains are best for controlled expansion and penetration at these speeds.

The reason I favor this particular combination of weight and speed is for close-range bullet performance. In the thicket I want a good exit wound with every shot. My shots are usually angling downward sharply from a treestand vantage point, and I want to knock the deer completely off his feet if at all possible. Should he travel at all, I want a

Barrel length and gun weight are considerations in thickets, and equally so for use from treestands. This is the Model Seven Remington, one of the author's personal favorites. (Photo by Judd Cooney)

blood trail that I can find blindfolded. For this reason I do not favor the little sizzlers like the 6mm Remington or .243 Winchester. I'm not knocking them; both are great deer calibers. However, their light, fast bullets are explosive at close range and are prone to stay in the deer rather than

The secret to thicket hunting is timing—knowing when to shoot so you can "thread the needle" and get your bullet through the brush and into the vitals of your buck. (Photo by Judd Cooney)

exit. I deem exit wounds essential when hunting thick cover where a few bounds may put the deer out of your sight in terrain that requires tracking on hands and knees. I want to recover every deer I shoot with as little fuss as possible.

Bullet design plays an important role in good penetration. In factory ammunition I have found the Winchester Silvertips to be extremely reliable in producing good exits. Similarly impressive are Federal's Hi-Shok bullets and Hornady Custom factory ammo loaded with Hornady Interlock bullets. Of course, excellent results will be achieved with "premium" loads featuring bullets such as Nosler Partitions, Trophy Bonded Bearclaws, Barnes X-Bullets, and Swift A-Frames.

The handloader probably has less reason to load for a thicket rifle than for any other kind of hunting because of the close range shooting; factory ammo will deliver more than acceptable accuracy and performance. However, reloaders will certainly do well to use bullets such as Silvertips, Nosler Partitions, Hornady Interlocks, Speer Grand Slams, or any of the other bullets mentioned above in their handloads. All are capable of good expansion and complete penetration.

Some might argue that heavy magnum rifles would do the same job, even at close range. This I would not argue. But magnums tend to lose velocity as the barrel is shortened to a greater degree than the calibers I have suggested. If you want the ideal thicket rifle, a long-barrelled magnum will be a cumbersome tool for the job, and nobody in his right mind wants to saw four inches off the barrel of his long-range magnum just to hunt the brush!

Here's an interesting comparison between the .300 Winchester Magnum and the .308 Winchester. The .300 magnum, with a 24-inch barrel and firing a spitzer 180-grain bullet, will deliver about 2562 foot-pounds of energy at 200 yards. The .308, with the same bullet but a 20-inch barrel, will deliver about the same energy at the muzzle. The .308 will land with virtually all of that energy at the short ranges required of a thicket rifle—and clearly that's more than plenty of energy for any whitetail deer.

What this means, in practical hunting terms, is that a .300 magnum, as a deer rifle, is of more value in terms of extended range than in extra foot-pounds needed to kill deer. At close range, as experienced when hunting the thickets, large magnums are of little practical value since, up close, you simply don't need the extra foot-pounds they deliver.

Recoil is certainly another factor to consider when hunting from treestands. I, for one, am not particularly intrigued by the idea of being kicked out from under my hat while perched 20 feet off the ground. Along with moderate bullet speed, I also believe in moderate recoil—which the calibers I mentioned, among others, certainly deliver. I have chosen the .308 Winchester as the ideal thicket rifle for my own personal hunting. I am continually amazed at the knockdown power of this little cartridge. When using 180-grain bullets in the .308, I seldom have a deer take more than a single step after I pull the trigger—and I get consistent exit wounds.

I have two thicket rifles. One is a Ruger Model 77RL Ultra Light weighing in at seven pounds, including scope and factory walnut stock. The overall length of the rifle is 40 inches. The other is a Remington Model Seven FS (for fiberglass stock). It comes from the factory with a synthetic stock, overall length of just 37½ inches, and weighs just 6½ pounds *with scope*! Both rifles have performed admirably for me over the years; dropping not only whitetails but also moose and bear in their tracks. A friend of mine borrowed my Remington .308 for a moose hunt in the Yukon and dropped a huge record-book bull with a single shot from the stubby little 18½-inch barrel. That leaves little doubt that it's enough gun for any whitetail on Earth!

For many hunters, a brush gun must be a fast shootin' carbine that enables them to sling as much lead as possible

A short, maneuverable, and highly accurate rifle is the ultimate thicket gun. A low fixed power or low-end variable scope is most ideal for thicket rifles.

at deer busting through the timber at close range. In my humble opinion, this approach to shooting deer would probably be best accomplished with a 12-gauge stoked with buckshot. For the satisfaction of making a clean, precise one-shot kill, I will ambush my buck with a thicket rifle capable of splitting hairs in the thickest deer haunts on Earth.

Every sensible article I've ever read on the perfect deer rifle concluded that there is no *one* perfect deer rifle for all existing hunting conditions. This writer is in total agreement with that fact, but as regards a perfect *thicket* rifle, I am very specific. A good thicket rifle is a precision tool for a very special type of hunting, and I find great satisfaction in using the right tool for the right job.

INDEX

Note: Bold page numbers indicaqte illustrations or photos.

Aiello, Joe, **7**
Alberta
    climate, 65
    forage, 59
    hunting methods, 63
    hunting regulations, 9-11, 60, 62-
        63, 65-66, 69
    hunting season, 63-64, 69
    hunting statistics, 51, 66-69
    outfitters/guides, 62, 65, 69
    rifle/caliber for, 64-65
    topography, 57, 59-60
    trophy areas, 51-55, **55**, 57, 60
    whitetail population, **54,** 69
    whitetail range, 52-54, **53, 55**
ammunition, **187**
    caliber selection, 25, 185-88, 197-
        98, 202-6
        Alberta, 64-65
        British Columbia, 43
        Manitoba, 91-92
        Saskatchewan, 83-84
    clearing customs, 30, 32
    reloading, 205
antler rattling
    Alberta, 63
    British Columbia, 46
    clothing, 169, 171
    cold weather, 135
    productivity of, 165-66
    Saskatchewan, 76, 78
    sites,, 166-68
    technique, 166, 171-79, **177, 178**
    treestand, **170,** 176-77, 179
antlers
    irregular, 57
    transporting, 30, 102
    trophy, 8

bag, hunting, 119, 121, 123, **133**

baiting, 148-54
    Saskatchewan, 79-80
barley, 150-52
Bean, Randy, **103**
blind, ground, **20,** 46, 63
boot blankets, **112,** 113
    covers, 113-14, **114**
boots, **109,** 110-16, **111, 115**
bowhunting, 16, 125
    Alberta, 65-66, 68, 69
    British Columbia, 49
    Manitoba, 90, 96, 98, 100-101, 103-
        5
    salt baiting and, 148-49
    Saskatchewan, 71-72, 78, 86, 87
Brewster, James, 36 (caption)
British Columbia
    climate, 36, 37-38, 39-40
    forage, 36-37, 38, 40-41
    hunting methods, 46
    hunting regulations, 42-43, 49
    hunting season, 45-46, 49
    hunting statistics, 41-42, 49
    outfitters/guides, 42-43, 46, 48, 49
    predation, 38-39, 41
    rifle/caliber for, 43
    topography, 35-36, 40-41
    trophy areas, **39,** 43-45, 49
    whitetail population, 35-36, 37-39,
        38, 40
    whitetail range, 35-36, **37**
Brown, Jack, **99**
buck, trophy-class, 7-8, 11-14
    See also trophy areas
bullets. *See* ammunition

calling, deer, 134-35
capes
    transporting, 30-31, 102
caps, 117, 119, **120, 126,** 127, **128**

circulation drive, 154-63, **155**
climate, 11-12
   Alberta, 65
   British Columbia, 36, 37-38, 39-40
   Manitoba, 101, 102-3
   Saskatchewan, 80-82
clothing
   for antler rattling, 169, 171
   boot blanket covers, 113-14, **114**
   boot blankets, **112**, 113
   boots, **109**, 110-16, **111**, **115**
   caps, 117, 119, **120**, **126**, 127, **128**
   cold weather, 25, 107-30, **120**
   dress code, 78-79, 96, 101
   foot warmers, **130**
   gloves, 123, 125
   hand warmers, 121, **122**, 123-25, **124**, **130**
   head/neck/face warmers, **126**, 127, **128**, 129
   hunting bag, 119, 121, 123, **133**
   jackets, 117, 119, 120
   manufacturers, 136-37
   overalls, 117, 119, **120**
   socks, 110, 114
   stock adjustment for, 131
   tree shirts, 129
   underwear, 117, **118**, 119
   vest, 117, 119, **120**
corn, 150-51
costs
   Anti-Freeze clothing system, 119
   boot blanket covers, 114
   boots, 111
   face mask, 127
   handwarmers, 123, 125
   hunt, 14, 23, 84
   hunting bag, 123
   license
      Alberta, 69
      British Columbia, 49
      Manitoba, 105
      Saskatchewan, 87
   synthetic stocks, 132
   tree shirt, 129
   underwear, 117
Courtice, Neal, 66 (Caption)
customs
   Canadian, 29-30
   Form 4457, 32
   U.S., 30-32

Delaronde, Ben, 90 (caption)
Dempsey, Carmen, 40 (caption)
documents, export, 30
drives, deer, 46, 139-48
   baiting, 148-54
   circulation, 154-63, **155**
Dwernychuck, Dean, **61**, 68

face mask, **126**, 127
firearms
   clearing customs, 29-30, 32
   preparing for cold, 130-32
   proof of origin, 32
   See also gun, rifle
forage
   Alberta, 59
   British Columbia, 36-37, 38, 40-41
   Manitoba, 96, 100-103
   Saskatchewan, 77
Froma, Jerry, **59**, 67

genetics, 11, 45
gloves, 123, 125
   See also warmers, hand
guides. *See* outfitters/guides
gun
   brush, 197-98, **201**
   -case, **31**
   hand-, 29
   shot-, 29-30, 84
   thicket, 197-208, **202**
   weight, 200
   See also firearms, rifle

Halko, Danny, **82**
Hanna, Cliff, **64**
Hansen, Milo, 68
Hansen, Shane, **64**
Harris, George, 104
Harris, Ken, **66**
Harrison, Phillip, **174**
Hawkins, Ken, 104
Hindbo, Susan, 121
Hryhoruk, Ted, 95 (caption)
hunt
   booking, 19-26
   cost, 14, 23, 84
   guaranteed, 25

industry, hunting, 5-6, 9-11
   eastern provinces, 14-15

jackets, 117, 119, **120**
Jackson, Ray, 44
Jansen, Stephen, **62,** 68

Kelbert, Dave, 83
Klinger, Doug, 58 (caption), 67
Koberstein, Ed., **56,** 66
Kotter, Elburn, 86 (caption)
Kress, Bob, **44**

license, hunting
    Alberta, 66, 69
    British Columbia, 42, 49
    Manitoba, 102, 105
    Saskatchewan, 84, 87
Lintott, Lloyd, 94 (caption)

Manitoba
    climate, 101, 102-3
    forage, 96, 100-101
    hunting methods, 92-93, 95-6, 98,
        100-101, 103-4
    hunting regulations, 96, 98, 100-
        102, 105
    hunting season, 100, 101, 105
    hunting statistics, 103-4, 105
    outfitters/guides, 102, 105
    rifle/caliber for, 91-92
    topography, 89-91
    trophy area, **93,** 104, 105
    whitetail population, 89-91, **92,**
        102-3
    whitetail range, 89-91, **91**
Marek, Paul, **81,** 83
McDonald, Larry, 90 (caption)
McGarvey, Don, **52,** 66
meat
    transporting, 30-32, 102
methods, hunting
    Alberta, 63
    British Columbia, 46
    Manitoba, 92-93, 95-96, 98, 100-
        101, 103-4
    of outfitters, 21-23
    Saskatchewan, 76, 78, 84-85
mittens, 123
    See also warmers, hand
Morin, Neil, **57,** 67
movement, deer, 46, 139-48
    with baiting, 148-54
    with circulation drives, 154-63, **155**
    monitoring, 149-50

    reasons for, 154
Murray, Eric, 104

New Brunswick, 14
"NO HANDGUNS" law, 29
noise
    fabric/tree bark, 129
    leaves, 168
    sling, 134
    synthetic stocks, 132
    treestand grate, 113-14
Nova Scotia, 14

outfitters/guides
    Alberta, 9-11, 62, 65, 69
    British Columbia, 42-43, 46, 48, 49
    eastern provinces, 14-15
    Manitoba, 102, 105
    Saskatchewan, 82, 84, 87
    selecting, 19-26
overalls, 117, 119, **120**

population, whitetail
    Alberta, **54,** 69
    British Columbia, 35-36, 37-39, **38,**
        40
    Manitoba, 89-91, **92,** 102-3
    Saskatchewan, 72, **74,** 74-76
predation, 38-39, 41

Race, Gene, **97**
range, whitetail
    Alberta, 52-54, **53, 55**
    British Columbia, 35-36, **37,** 38
    Manitoba, 89-91, **91**
    Saskatchewan, **72**
ratio
    buck/doe, 75-76, 78, 87
    fawn/adult, 35
regulations, hunting
    Alberta, 9-11, 60, 62-63, 65-66, 69
    British Columbia, 42-43, 49
    Manitoba, 96, 98, 100-102, 105
    Saskatchewan, **73,** 77-80, 82, 87
rifle
    accuracy, 199-200
    bolt action vs. semiauto, 195
    caliber selection, 25, 185-88, 197-
        98, 202-6
        Alberta, 64-65
        British Columbia, 43
        Manitoba, 91-92

Saskatchewan, 83-84
clearing customs, 29-30, 32
long-range, 181-95, **184**, **187**
preparing for cold, 130-32
recoil, 206
scope, 183-84, 188-93, 200-201
slings, 132-34
thicket, 197-208, **201**, **202**
triggers, 189, 201-2
weight, 200
rut, 15-16, 46, 63, 101
baiting during, 152

salt
as bait, 148-49
on capes, 31
sanctuaries, 154-63, **155**
Saskatchewan
climate, 80-82
forage, 77
hunting methods, 76, 78, 84-85
hunting regulations, **73**, 77-80, 82,
87
hunting season, 78-79, 84, 87
hunting statistics, 74-75, 87
outfitters/guides, 82, 84, 87
rifle/caliber for, 83-84
topography, 72-74, 76-77
trophy area, 74-75, **75**, 87
whitetail population, 72, **74**, 74-76
whitetail range, **72**
scope
long-range rifle, 183-84, 188-93,
191, **192**, **194**
thicket gun, 200-201
season, hunting, 15-16
Alberta, 63-64, 69
British Columbia, 45-46, 49
Manitoba, 100, 101, 105
Saskatchewan, 78-79, 84, 87
shirt, tree, 129
sign, **26**, **41**, 149-50, 168-69
skins
transporting, 30-31, 102
sling, rifle, 132-34
socks, 110, 114
statistics, hunting
Alberta, 51, 66-69
British Columbia, 41-42, 49
Manitoba, 103-4, 105
Saskatchewan, 74-75, 87
Stein, Brian, **83**

Stewart, Darcy, **13**
stocks
manufacturer, 137
synthetic, **131**, 131-32, 201
Strachan, Murry, 104
Swiston, Peter, **79**

target, silhouette, 182-84, 190-93
Temple, Robert, **85**
topography
Alberta, 57, 59-60
British Columbia, 35, 36, 40-41
eastern provinces, 14
Manitoba, 89-91
Saskatchewan, 72-74, 76-77
treestand, 46, 63, 101, 129-30
antler rattling, **170**, 176-77, 179
bag, 119, 121, 123, **133**
triggers, rifle, 189, 201-2
trophy areas, 11
Alberta, 51-55, **55**, 57, 60
British Columbia, **39**, 43-45, 49
Manitoba, **93**, 104, 105
Saskatchewan, 74-75, **75**

underwear, 117, **118**, 119

venison
transporting, 30-32, 102
vests, 117, 119, **120**

Warkentin, Ken, 100
warmers
foot, **130**
hand, 121, **122**, 123-25, **124**, **130**
head/neck/face, **126**, 127, **128**, 129
weather, cold
antler rattling, 135
deer calling, 134-35
dressing, 107-30
firearm preparation, 130-32
weather, warm, 16, 30-31
salt baiting, 148
wind, 167-68, 169
winter kills, 11-12
British Columbia, 37-38
Manitoba, 102-3
Saskatchewan, 75
Woods, Kevin, **40**

WHITETAIL SECRETS
VOLUME FIVE — HUNTING THE CANADIAN GIANT

Black and white photography by Russell Thornberry

Color photography by Ian McMurchy:
Pages 4, 18, 34, 50, 70, 88, 107, 196

Color photography by Judd Cooney:
Page 28

Color photography by Charles Alsheimer:
Pages 138, 164

Color photography by Russell Thornberry:
Page 180

Illustrated by David Baer

Designed by Kirby J. Kiskadden

Text composed in Berkeley by
E. T. Lowe Publishing Co., Nashville, Tennessee

Color Separations and Film prepared by
D&T Bailey, Nashville, Tennessee

Printed and Bound by
Quebecor Printing, Kingsport, Tennessee

Text sheets are acid-free Warren Flo Book
by S. D. Warren Company

Endleaves are Rainbow Parchment by Ecological Fibers, Inc.

Cover material is Taratan II Bonded Leather by Cromwell